The complete guide to

Citing Government Documents

A manual for writers & librarians

by Diane L. Garner and Diane H. Smith
Pennsylvania State University Libraries

for the Government Documents Round Table,
American Library Association

Congressional Information Service, Inc.
Bethesda, MD

CIS Staff

Director of Communications: Richard K. Johnson

Project Manager: Marcia Taylor

Design and Production: Liz Kuny

Proofreading: Maria Brown, Caryl Dikkers, Helene Gaffney, Victoria E. King,
Elizabeth Naccarato, Ruth Sowash, Leslie Wilson, Pat Wyler, Sheila Young

Printing Services: Lee Mayer

Proceeds from the sale of this publication go to support the activities of the Government Documents Round Table, American Library Association.

Library of Congress Cataloging in Publication Data

Garner, Diane L.
  The complete guide to citing government documents.

  Bibliography: p.
  Includes index.
  1. Government publications—Bibliography—Methodology. 2. Bibliographical citations.
I. Smith, Diane H. II. American Library Association. Government Documents Round Table.
III. Title. IV. Title: Citing government documents.
Z7164.G7G37 1984 [J9.5] 016.015 84-11357
ISBN 0-88692-023-X

Printed in the U.S.A.

Preface

This manual is designed to fill a void in the literature of citation/style manuals and librarianship. Numerous books describe how to write a bibliography or a footnote (see Appendix A), but when they deal with government documents, it is usually on a very superficial level. These style manuals do not discuss the varying document formats and, for the most part, the authors of these texts seem to know little about the sources and types of documents or the access points important for document location.

In the hope of solving this dilemma we have written this manual outlining document citation. We have prepared it from the perspective that a bibliographic citation has four purposes. First, it should *identify* and *differentiate* an item for a reader. Second, it should give a reader some indication of the intellectual *quality* (i.e. a major study as opposed to an informational pamphlet) of the items cited. Third, it should give *credit* to the ideas of other authors, as applicable. Fourth, it should help the reader *locate* the cited item. We feel that all of these purposes have equal value, and have tried to remain true to the objectives of a citation, given the publishing and distribution practices of government entities.

In determining which elements should and should not be present in a document citation, we have used their value as a reference access point as our touchstone. If the information would not help a person locate a document or if it did not provide information about the item's format, we have not included it.

Stylistically, we have tried to conform as much as possible, given our reference perspective, to ANSI bibliographic standards. Our goal is for this manual to supplement, not replace, standard style/citation manuals (i.e. Chicago, MLA, Turabian, etc.). That way a person writing a bibliography composed of documents and other monographic and serial sources will have a consistent form. We do realize, however, that occasionally certain styles (in particular, legal citations) are required by schools or publishers. When this is the case, we would encourage our readers to review and use the style that is required in that particular circumstance.

In a more general sense, we would also like to stress that content

iii

should never be sacrificed to style. We would urge our readers not to become excessively concerned with the mechanics of a citation. While we would never say that style is unimportant, we would say that the anxiety caused by the demand for a *correct form* is entirely out of proportion to its worth. Furthermore, when the quest for correct form causes one to omit necessary content, the integrity of the citation is sacrificed. While punctuation, capitalization, spacing, etc. are important, they can be modified, as necessary, to ensure clarity of content.

This manual is written for three primary audiences: writers, general reference librarians, and government documents specialists. To meet the needs of each, we have discussed the function of various types of documents and the bibliographic elements necessary to them, and offered our rationale for the inclusion or omission of specific elements. We have also detailed the problems arising from the quirks of government publishing, and provided clear examples to deal with them. A glossary has been included for clarification of terms, as well as an index for quick access to particular types of citation problems.

When we began this manual we had no idea of the amount of time it would consume, both ours and that of our fellow staff members and friends. As the hours and weeks accumulated, it became obvious that profuse thanks and acknowledgements were due to all who had helped us with our project. First, we wish to thank the patient and supportive documents staff at the Pennsylvania State University Libraries. They not only encouraged us, but took on extra desk hours and tasks while we disappeared to debate citation elements. We are especially grateful to Anne Stine, who took our handwritten thoughts and typed them into a readable text. Her patience was extraordinary, surviving the countless times we asked her to change page after page. Second, we thank our friend Nancy Cline, who took time to read the manuscript and made substantial remarks about it. Finally, we wish to acknowledge the support and input of the American Library Association's Government Documents Round Table (GODORT), without whose help this manual probably could not have been published.

Diane L. Garner
Diane H. Smith

List of Illustrations

Table of Contents

Chapter 1

Introduction

Purposes of a Citation

A citation can serve a number of purposes. The first is a matter of honesty: you should give credit to the people from whom you got your material. A citation can also lend authority to your work, signaling your reader that a great deal of careful research went into your final product. The last, and perhaps most important, function of a citation is to provide a kind of road map for research. This is the function with which most libraries, and this manual, are primarily concerned.

A good citation should give your readers enough accurate and pertinent bibliographic information so that they can locate what you have cited. This will depend partly on the work cited and partly on the methods of access used by libraries. The problem is that library methods are not absolutely uniform. The best you can do in creating a citation is to provide enough information to accommodate most known situations. The usual citation — author, title, place, publisher, date — while adequate in most libraries for many books, is not adequate for government documents.

What Are Government Documents?

A government document may be anything printed (or otherwise reproduced) by or for a governmental body. A government document may be a pamphlet on how to quit smoking, a transcript of a hearing, an expert's

1

report on the food needs of a developing country, the design of a municipal water system, a collection of statistics about the population of an area, the debates of a parliament: in short, any part of the activities of a governmental body which the government chooses to record and make available.

Why do government documents present special citation problems? There are many reasons, but basically they all come down to this: governments do not always follow standard publishing practices, and libraries do not always treat documents as they treat books.

Government Publishing Practices

In the case of commercial publications, certain publishing practices are well-established. You typically can expect to find a page with an obvious title, author, place of publication, and publisher. On the back of that page you can find a copyright date. Governments, however, do not necessarily follow these "rules."

In the first place, many government documents are not meant for publication in the usual sense. Although the government may make every effort to ensure wide distribution, the majority of government documents result from the government's "business" and not from a desire to publish something. Thus, the publication style is developed independently by each agency with a view to its own needs rather than to a uniform style.

Secondly, many government documents lack, in part or in full, the elements considered necessary for a good citation, i.e. author, title, and imprint. Many documents have only anonymous authors. Title is the one bibliographic element most likely to be found (though not always), but even title can be a problem. For example, the design of a document may present you with several choices as to title, or the title may be so long and rambling that it is useless. The imprint — place and publisher especially — is the element most likely to be missing altogether. If you follow the usual citation style and simply omit what is not given on the document, you may be left with nearly useless bits of information.

Library Document Collections

If government publishing practices have made document citations difficult, libraries and those whose catalogs and indexes serve libraries have not made them any easier. When a library receives a book, it prepares bibliographic records filed by author, title, and subject. In contrast, when a library receives a document (especially a library which receives large numbers of documents), it more than likely will keep the document in a separate collection and make no public bibliographic records at all.

This situation has been relieved somewhat in recent years and for some kinds of documents by the creation of special indexing books, but the fact still remains that there is nothing resembling a typical library card catalog for government documents in which you can find a comprehensive and cumulative list — by author, title, and subject — of what a library has. Furthermore, even in those cases where a library has given a document a complete bibliographic record, that record is often so complicated that it is only by chance that one ever comes across it in the file.

Instead of cataloging documents like books, libraries have relied on other ways of making them accessible. For a document citation to be useful it must take into account these other ways. These include specialized book catalogs, abstracts, and indexes in which bibliographic records may be found by date, by document or report numbers, by names of agencies or committees, by keywords in titles, and so on.

Mechanics of a Citation

The elements of a complete citation could include any or all of the following: author, title, edition, imprint, series, and notes. A document citation has the same elements except that issuing agency takes the place of an author. Within these categories various kinds of data should be included, depending on their relevance to a particular document (Table 1).

The sequence of these bibliographic elements and the sequence of data within these elements follow ANSI standards (with modifications). On the assumption that few bibliographies will consist of only government documents, we have kept to a form which is compatible with other traditional forms while at the same time providing slots in which to put information necessary to the retrieval of government documents.

All of the data listed in Table 1 could not possibly be used in a single citation. Therefore, there is no point in trying to determine the sequence of the data if every one were used. There is value, however, in showing the sequence in the "worst" cases.

A cursory look at Table 1 will show that only issuing agency, title, and notes have enough possible components to make their construction complex. Of these the title element presents the most difficulties. The order of data in the issuing agency element is fairly well-established by hierarchy. The order of data in the notes element is relatively flexible: it does not make much difference what order you use as long as you use it consistently. It remains, then, to consider the sequence of data in the title element.

Table 1

CITATION ELEMENTS

Issuing Agency

Political Affiliation
Agency Name
Sub-Agency Name
Number Designator of
  Parliamentary Body
Meeting Place of a
  Parliamentary Body

Title

Title
Abbreviated Title
Subtitle
Date
Place of Meeting
Date of Meeting
Number of Meeting
Personal Author
Personal Author Affiliation
  and Place
Non-Governmental Corporate
  Author
Document Type
Document Number
Report Number
Medium Designator
Patent Title
Patentee
Patent Number
Patent Date
Number of Part
Volume/Issue Number
Pagination

Edition

Edition Statement
Party Responsible for Revisions

Imprint

Place
  – City
  – State/Province/District
  – Country
Publisher
  – Name
  – Co-Publisher
Date
  – Date of Publication
  – Date of Copyright
  – Date of Issuance

Series

Series Title
Series Number
Multiple Series Titles

Notes

Distribution Source
Format
  – Looseleaf
  – Mimeo
Superintendent of Documents
  Number
Microform Collection Title and
  Accession Number
Serial Set Volume Number
Joint Issuing Agency
Joint Sponsoring Body
UN Sales Number
ISBN/ISSN Number
Language of Work
Publication Type
Map Scale
Media Size

In spite of appearances in real citations the maximum number of parts in the title element is limited. Several data are mutually exclusive. A

Congressional hearing, for example, might have a date and place, but it would not have a personal author. The matrix shows data which might be used in a single citation and data which are mutually exclusive.

Geopolitical Designation. | Issuing Agency. | Subgroup, | Number Designator, | Meeting Place of Parliamentary Body. || Title: | Subtitle | Volume No. |

Personal Author | Corporate Author, | Place
or
Corporate Author, | Place
or ┤| (Report Number(s); |
Hearing, | Date
or
Conference Place, | Date

Medium). || Edition. || Place of Publication: | Publisher, | Date of Publication. || (Series). || (Notes).

The "worst case" we can imagine is given in Figure 1. It contains an example of nearly every element of data possible in a standard citation. However, it must be emphasized that this citation is an amalgam of

Issuing Agency —————————————┤ Subgroup of Issuing Agency
U.S. Environmental Protection Agency. Office of Research and
————————————┤ Subgroup of Subgroup of Issuing Agency —|| Title—
Development. Office of Environmental Engineering. *Energy*
————————————————┤ Date in Title | Subtitle —————————┤
Alternatives and the Environment, 1980: Handbook for Citizens by
Personal Authors ————————————————┤ Corporate Authors
John Jones, Herbert Phihl, and Anne Lewis of Citizens
————————————————┤ Place of Corporation | Agency Report Numbers
Energy Systems, Inc., Boston, Mass. (EPA 600/3-81-032;
————————————————┤ Medium —|| Edition —|| Place of Publication |
EPA-CPUB-80-28; microfiche). Rev. ed. Washington:
Publisher ————————————————┤ Date || Series —————————————
Government Printing Office, 1981. (Environmental Protection
————————————————┤ 2nd Series—————————————————||
Technology Series; Citizens Handbook Series No. 28).
Notes: SuDoc Number ——┤ Alternate Distribution ——————————||
(EP1.23/2:600/3-81-032; also available NTIS PB-80 103962).

Fig. 1

An Imaginary Beast: The Mythical Worst Case

several real citations plus a liberal dose of imagination. It is quite unlikely that such a document would exist in the real world. A more reasonable (and real) case is the citation to a NASA technical report which appears in Figure 2.

Issuing Agency————————————————————————‖ Title Proper—
U.S. National Aeronautics and Space Administration. *Environmental*
——|
Exposure Effects on Composite Materials for Commercial Aircraft by
Personal Authors————————————————————————| Corporate Author—
Martin N. Gibbons and Daniel J. Hoffman of Advanced Struc-
————————————————————————————| Place of Corporation | Report No.
tures, Boeing Commercial Airplane Co., Seattle, Wash. (NASA-
————————| Medium—‖ Place of Pub—| Publisher —————————————|
CR-3502; microfiche). Washington: Government Printing Office,
Date ‖ Notes: SuDoc No.—| Alternate Distribution —————————————————‖
1982. (NAS1.26:3502; also available NTIS NASA-CR-3502).

Fig. 2
Real Worst Case

A "double worst case" can occur when you are citing a part of a non-periodical publication, because you must give information both about the part and about the whole publication (Fig. 3). Simplify this problem

INSERTION IN HEARING

Corporate Author———‖ Title of Part ————————————————————————
Robins and Assoc. "Comparative Analysis of Sediment Pond Design
——
Requirements: Interim Versus Final Federal Regulations (June
—————————| Page Numbers ‖ Issuing Agency ————————————————————
13, 1979)," pp. 89-110. In U.S. Senate. Committee on Energy
————————————————————‖ Title————————————————————————
and Natural Resources. *Oversight — The Surface Mining Control and*
————————————————————| Hearing—| Date ———————————| Medium ——‖
Reclamation Act of 1977 Hearings, 19, 21 June 1979 (microfiche).
Place of Pub—| Publisher —————————————————| Date ‖ Note: SuDoc No.—‖
Washington: Government Printing Office, 1979. (Y4.En2:96-44).

PAPER IN PROCEEDINGS

Author of Part——‖ Title of Part ————————————————————————————|
Moghissi, A.A. "Biological Half Life of Tritium in Humans"
Report No. of Part——| Page Numbers ‖ Issuing Agency————————————
(IAEA-SM-232/65), pp. 501-507. In International Atomic Energy

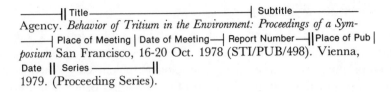

Agency. *Behavior of Tritium in the Environment: Proceedings of a Sym-*
posium San Francisco, 16-20 Oct. 1978 (STI/PUB/498). Vienna,
1979. (Proceeding Series).

Fig. 3
Worst Cases: Citation to a Part

by dividing the citation, citing first the part and then the whole. (For a
more detailed discussion, see US 7, SLR 7, and I 7.)

Personal Author. || "Title of Part: | Subtitle of Part | (Date of Part; | Report
Number of Part; | Medium of Part)," | Pagination. || In Issuing Agency. ||
Title of Whole: | Subtitle | Personal Author | Corporate Author, | Place
of Corporation | (Report Number of Whole; | Medium). || Edition. || Place
of Publication: | Publisher, | Date of Publication. || (Series). || (Notes —
SuDoc Number; | Alternate Distribution, etc.).

Needless complications can arise when you try to do too much with
a single citation. It is tempting, in citing an annual title over a number of
years, to include everything in one citation. This is possible only if there
are no changes in issuing agency, title, publication form and type,
publisher, or required notes. Few, if any, government publications meet
these requirements. Remember that you must cite the publication in
hand, not some generic title. Thus, for example, you would cite:

NOT

> U.S. Department of the Interior. *Annual Report* 1849-1962.
> Washington, 1849-1963.

BUT

> U.S. House. 31st Congress, 1st Session. *Report of the Secretary of the*
> *Interior, 1849* (H.Ex.Doc.5). Washington, 1849. (Serial Set 570).

and

> "Annual Report of the Secretary of the Interior," pp. 1-117. In
> U.S. Department of the Interior. *Reports of the Department of the*
> *Interior, 1913.* Washington: Government Printing Office, 1914.
> (I1.1:1913).

and

> U.S. Department of the Interior. *Annual Report of the Secretary of the*
> *Interior for the Fiscal Year Ending June 30, 1939.* Washington:
> Government Printing Office, 1939. (I1.1:1939).

Footnotes vs. Bibliography

All examples in the text are given in bibliographic form. There is no distinction for footnotes, since the differences between these two spring from printing styles rather than from bibliographic needs. When footnotes are printed at the bottom of a page of text, it looks better if you keep the indentations uniform and similar to the paragraph. Also, since footnotes are arranged by a number, there is no need to put an author's last name first as you do in a bibliography. With the modern practice of using end notes rather than footnotes, there is really no reason why the citation form of the two should differ. However, for the sake of those who wish to maintain a difference, Table 2 gives both forms for the three basic kinds of citations.

Table 2

CITATION FORMS

Citation to a Whole Work

BIBLIOGRAPHY

Issuing Agency Elements (in usual order). *Title Elements.*
  Edition. Place: Publisher, Date. (Series Elements). (Notes).

FOOTNOTE

Issuing Agency Elements (in usual order), *Title Elements.*
  Edition. (Place: Publisher, Date. (Series Elements).
  (Notes).) Page Numbers.

Citation to a Periodical Article

BIBLIOGRAPHY

Author of Article (name inverted). "Title of Article," *Title of
  Periodical* Volume:Issue(Date) Page Numbers. (Notes).

FOOTNOTE

Author (name in usual order), "Title of Article," *Title of
  Periodical* Volume:Issue(Date) Page Numbers. (Notes).

Citation to a Part

BIBLIOGRAPHY

Author (name inverted). "Title of Part," Page Numbers. In
  Issuing Agency Elements. *Title Elements.* Edition. Place:

Publisher, Date. (Series Elements). (Notes).

FOOTNOTE

Author (name in usual order), "Title of Part," Page
Numbers. In Issuing Agency Elements, *Title Elements.*
Edition. Place: Publisher, Date. (Series Elements). (Notes).

Citing a work in a footnote or in a bibliography depends on the use
being made of it. In general you would use a footnote to acknowledge and
identify material (quotations, data, ideas) taken directly from another
source or material which you need to substantiate your position. Usually,
a footnote cites a precise part of a work. A bibliography, on the other
hand, is a list of sources. It may be a list of all the sources consulted in
your research, or it may be a selective list of resources, depending on your
aims.

Successive Citations

The *same work* will be cited more than once only in footnotes. How you
handle these successive citations will depend on whether you have a bibliography in addition to footnotes. If you have only footnotes, you should
give a full citation the first time. After that, an abbreviated form is acceptable. If you have a bibliography, give the complete form in the
bibliography and use the short form in the footnotes.

The author's last name, a short title, and a page reference are used
in the typical abbreviated book citation. In a government document citation this translates as issuing agency, short title, and page number. (For
the full form of this citation see US 2.1b.)

AID. *Kitale Maize,* p. 3.

Shorten the issuing agency's name only if you can do so without
losing its identification. For example, U.S. Department of Housing and
Urban Development could safely be shortened to HUD for a second footnote reference, but U.S. House. Committee on Appropriations could *not*
be shortened to Appropriations Committee without confusion unless there
were no other references to documents of an Appropriations Committee.

When abbreviating a document title, make sure that you do not take
out so much information that your reader will not be able to distinguish
the original source. Once you have decided on a shortened form of both
issuing agency and title, be sure to use it consistently.

We do not recommend the use of Latin words and abbreviations
(*ibid., op. cit.* and *idem*) for successive citations, because they are too often

misused and misunderstood.

In a bibliography when the same issuing agency is listed in successive citations, you may substitute an eight-space underline followed by a period for the issuing agency's name. Be sure that the agency is exactly the same in all its divisions before you use this convention!

North Atlantic Treaty Organization. *The Eurogroup*. Brussels, [by 1982].

_____. *Financial and Economic Data Relating to NATO Defense* (Press Release M-DPC-2(82)24). Brussels, 1982. (1983 IIS microfiche 2220-S1).

Punctuation, Capitalization, and Abbreviations

Follow the punctuation given in our examples and in Table 2. Use periods between citation elements. Enclose report numbers and medium in parentheses within the title element.

Enclose the series and notes elements in parentheses. Brackets [ ] are used to tell your reader that the information was not on the document, but was derived or deduced in some way by you. Ellipses (. . .) indicate that words were omitted from a title. Titles of whole works are either underlined or italicized; exact titles taken from parts are enclosed in quotation marks, but working titles of parts are not.

In general, we recommend that you capitalize the issuing agency and author's name, titles, subtitles, imprint, and series or collection titles. Within these elements, do not capitalize articles, prepositions (of less than 5 letters), and conjunctions. Do not capitalize the medium, but do capitalize the first word in such elements as edition and notes. When dealing with foreign languages, follow the rules for the language of the document in hand.

In using abbreviations, choose a style and use it throughout. You may find a style in a manual, such as the *Chicago Manual of Style;* you may follow the examples in this manual; or you may (and usually must) follow a style prescribed by a publisher or institution for whom you are writing. We have generally used the *Chicago Manual of Style* in abbreviating state names and months. We use traditionally accepted abbreviations for Congressional documents:

House Document   – H.Doc.98-1
House Report   – H.Rpt.
House Executive Document   – H.Ex.Doc.
Senate Document   – S.Doc.

House Executive Report   – H.Ex.Rpt.
Senate Report   – S.Rpt.
Senate Executive Document   – S.Ex.Doc.
Senate Executive Report   – S.Ex.Rpt.

Other abbreviations are taken directly from the document in hand.

Plan Ahead

Be consistent. Look at the rules before you start out and stick to them. Remember that the purpose of a citation is to give your reader information. The function of a citation's mechanics is to make that information easy to read, and a consistent pattern is easier to read than a random one. We strove for consistency in our examples, and they should be used as a model for your citations.

Above all do not become excessively concerned with the mechanics of the citation. While we would not go so far as to say that form is unimportant, we would say that the anguish caused by the demand for a **correct form** is out of all proportion to its worth. Further, when the quest for correct form causes one to omit necessary content, the integrity of the citation is sacrificed.

You will save yourself a lot of work if you take careful notes while you are doing your research. When using indexes, take the bibliographic information, such as issuing agency, title, publisher, and date, from the index. Then you will not have to figure out the correct information from a confusing array of candidates. Furthermore, if you are taking the information from the standard documents indexes (see Appendix B), you can be sure that your reader will be able to find the documents you have cited.

Another source of help can be found in bibliographic forms printed in the document. These go by many names — bibliographic data sheet and cataloging in publication (CIP) are two of them. What they do is bring together the information needed for libraries' bibliographic records. In so doing they also give you the information you need for a citation. You will find these mainly in technical reports and in international documents, either in the front or the back of the document.

How To Use This Manual

The text is divided into three chapters: U.S. federal, state-local-regional, and international documents. Many of the problems encountered in these three groups are similar. However, there are always problems or types of documents unique to each group. We have tried to arrange the discussion and examples so that both the general and the particular could be covered in an orderly fashion. Most of the examples given are for real documents, but, when we could not readily find examples in our collection of cases that we knew from experience to be a problem, we did not hesitate to create plausible citations.

The U.S. chapter is the model for the SLR (state, local, regional) and I (International) chapters. It is the longest and most detailed because, in most U.S. libraries, U.S. federal documents represent the largest collection with the greatest use. Rather than repeat ourselves at length we refer the reader to the U.S. chapter for some of the justifications for why we do what we do.

In each chapter the citation elements are discussed and illustrated in the sequence in which they occur in a citation. Each example and its accompanying text are numbered in outline form. Within each chapter there may be some variations on the basic outline in order to accommodate particular problems.

Both the Table of Contents and the Index will lead you to the section in the manual that discusses your particular concern. The Index covers titles of well-known documents and document types (e.g., UN mimeos). In addition, and perhaps most important, it includes common problems (e.g., what to do with report numbers).

You will find the Index a quick way of getting to the information you need. We do recommend that you read the section(s) relating to the document you have in hand, particularly when you have no idea of how to cite it. We believe you will find our explanations useful, although in most cases the example will probably be sufficient. If not, determine which citation element in your document does not fit the pattern in the example. Then, go back to the Index or consult the Table of Contents for the location of the discussion of that element.

Chapter 2

United States Documents

U.S. documents are publications either written or sponsored by the federal government. These publications cover a variety of subjects and formats. They may be as lengthy and as important as the Warren Commission Report on the assassination of John F. Kennedy or as ephemeral as a poster introducing the latest commemorative postage stamp. The form of U.S. documents may be the traditional ink on paper, microform, audiovisual, or electronic data.

US 1   **ISSUING AGENCY**

For a U.S. document cite the issuing agency as the first element, rather than a personal author. The reasons for this are:

1) indexing until recently did not consistently use personal author;

2) indicating the U.S. government instead of a personal author will alert your reader immediately to the fact that you are citing a government document;

3) most libraries with documents collections have them classified by government agency and can more easily

and quickly locate the document if the issuing agency is apparent.

The two exceptions to the rule of citing the issuing agency as the author occur when you are citing a part of a publication or a technical report. (See US 7 and US 8.28 for a description of how to construct such author statements.)

US 1.1   Single Issuing Agency

For U.S. documents begin with "U.S.," followed by the name of the agency in hierarchical order. The object of this part of the citation is to describe the issuing agency so that anybody with a standard government reference source (such as the *U.S. Government Manual*) can identify it.

> U.S. Civil Rights Commission. *Immigration Issues in Hawaii.* Washington: Government Printing Office, 1979. (CR1.2:H31).

US 1.1a   If the agency given on the document is composed of many bureaucratic levels, how do you decide which ones to include? Usually you need use only the "umbrella" department and the lowest level agency given.

> U.S. Department of Labor. Employment Standards Administration. *Groups with Historically High Incidences of Unemployment.* Washington: Government Printing Office, 1980. (L36.12:980).

US 1.1b   An agency which is well-known in its own right does not need to be preceded by its departmental name.

> U.S. Forest Service. *Taraghee Lodgepole: A Pioneering Effort in Deadwood Salvage.* Washington: Government Printing Office, 1979. (A13.2:T17).

US 1.1c   When in doubt, include everything. When you include more than one level of the agency, do it in order of largest to smallest.

> U.S. Environmental Protection Agency. Office of Research and Development. Office of Environmental Engineering and Technology. *Energy Alternatives and the Environment: 1979* (EPA-600/9-80-009). n.p., 1979.

US 1.2   **Multiple Issuing Agencies**

If the document has more than one issuing agency (Fig. 4), use the first one listed. This agency will be noted in the standard indexes as the issuing agency, and it will help your reader locate the document.

> U.S. Employment and Training Administration. *Environmental Protection Careers Guidebook.* Washington: 1980.

US 1.3   **Congress as Issuing Agency**

For Congressional publications, you do not need to include "Congress" in the hierarchical order since there is only one U.S. House or Senate.

> U.S. House. Committee on Interior and Insular Affairs. *Entitled the "California Wilderness Act of 1983"* (H.Rpt.98-40). Washington: Government Printing Office, 1983. (Y1.1/8:98-40).

US 1.3a   The one exception is when citing a joint Congressional committee publication. In this case you must use "U.S. Congress. Joint Committee on ..." to alert your reader to the fact that the item is Congressional.

> U.S. Congress. Joint Economic Committee. *High Technology and Regional Development* Hearing, 1 Mar. 1982. Washington: Government Printing Office, 1982. (Y4.Ec7:T22/4).

US 1.3b   If, for alphabetizing purposes, you wish to keep all Congressional publications together, you may use "U.S. Congress. House." or "U.S. Congress. Senate."

> U.S. Congress. Senate. *Year-end Report of the 2nd Session of the 97th Congress* (S.Doc.97-38). Washington: Government Printing Office, 1982. (Y1.1/3:97-38).

US 1.3c   For committee prints, hearings, or reports use only the name of the main committee as the issuing agency, not that of any subcommittee. These types of documents are listed under the name of the main committee in the standard indexes and are arranged in most libraries by these committees.

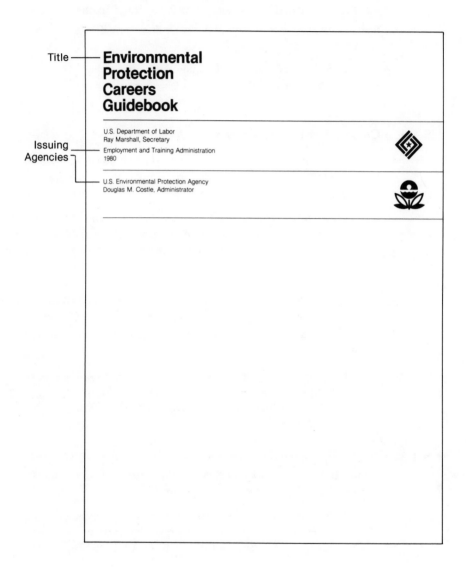

Title —— **Environmental Protection Careers Guidebook**

U.S. Department of Labor
Ray Marshall, Secretary

Issuing Agencies —— Employment and Training Administration
1980

U.S. Environmental Protection Agency
Douglas M. Costle, Administrator

Fig. 4
U.S. Document: Title Page

COMMITTEE PRINTS

U.S. Senate. Special Committee on Aging. *Heat Stress and Older Americans: Problems and Solutions* (S.Prt.98-76). Washington: Government Printing Office, 1983. (Y4.Ag4:S.Prt.98-76).

HEARINGS

U.S. House. Committee on the Judiciary. *Racially Motivated Violence* Hearings, 4 Mar., 3 June, 12 Nov. 1981 (Serial No. 135). Washington: Government Printing Office, 1983. (Y4.J89/1:97/135).

REPORTS

U.S. House. Committee on the Judiciary. *Shipping Act of 1983* (H.Rpt.98-53, Pt. 2). Washington: Government Printing Office, 1983. (Y1.1/8:98-53/Pt.2).

US 1.3d With conference reports you cannot cite a single committee. Use instead the Congressional chamber issuing the report.

U.S. House. *Authorizing Appropriations for Fiscal Years 1982 and 1983 for the Department of State, the United States Information Agency, and the Board for International Broadcasting* Conference Report (H.Rpt.97-693). Washington: Government Printing Office, 1982. (Y.1.1/3:97-693).

US 1.3e For Congressional "documents" the issuing agency is either "U.S. Senate" or "U.S. House," with no committee designation. These publications are in fact the product of the entire Congressional chamber, not of a committee.

U.S. Senate. *Dangerous Stalemate: Superpower Relations in Autumn 1983* (S.Doc.98-16). Washington: Government Printing Office, 1983. (Y1.1/3:98-16).

US 1.3f Acts, bills, and resolutions are numbered sequentially in the chamber in which they originate with no indication of the Congress. In order to avoid making your reader look in 98 Congresses (and 98 indexes) for a bill, you should identify the number and the session of the Congress as part of the issuing agency (Fig. 9).

ACTS

U.S. House. 97th Congress, 1st Session. *H.R. 1946,*

> *An Act to Reinstate and Validate . . . Oil and Gas Leases
> . . . OCS-P-0218 and OCS-P-226.* Washington: Gov-
> ernment Printing Office, 1981. (GPO microfiche
> no. 393, coordinate C13).

BILLS

> U.S. House. 96th Congress, 1st Session. *H.R. 2,
> A Bill to Require Authorization for Budget Authority . . . .*
> Washington: Government Printing Office, 1979.
> (GPO microfiche no. 1, coordinate A3).

RESOLUTIONS

> U.S. Senate. 97th Congress, 1st Session. *S.Res. 148,
> Resolution . . . for a Moratorium on the Commercial Killing
> of Whales.* Washington: Government Printing Office,
> 1982. (GPO microfiche no. 24, coordinate A1).

US 2   TITLE

The title of a document, just like the title of a book, is usually
obvious. However, due to graphic design and document
organization, the title may be "hidden," or there may be some
confusion as to what actually constitutes the title. For your
readers' convenience, you should use the same title that
indexes use. If you found the document by using one of the
standard sources (Appendix B), use the title as given there.

US 2.1   Location of Title

If you must decide on your own what the title is, first look at
the title page of the document and choose whatever title seems
most prominent and provides the most revealing description of
the document. Only the title proper should be underlined, as
indicated by italics in these examples.

> U.S. Department of Health, Education and Welfare.
> John L. Fogarty International Center for Advanced
> Study in the Health Sciences. *Barefoot Doctor's
> Manual.* Washington: Government Printing Office,
> 1974. (HE20.3708:B23).

US 2.1a   Sometimes, especially in technical literature, you will see a
form entitled "Bibliographic Data Sheet" or "Technical
Report Documentation Page" (Fig. 5). Since this form is

Type of
Document

Grant/
Contract
Number

Agency
Report
Number

Title

Personal
Author

Contracting
Organization

Issuing/
Sponsoring
Agency

Technical Report Documentation Page

1. Report No. CG-D-66-80	2. Government Accession No.	3. Recipient's Catalog No.
4. Title and Subtitle A Simulator Study of Deepwater Port Shiphandling and Navigation Problems in Poor Visibility		5. Report Date January 1981
		6. Performing Organization Code
7. Author's) R. C. Cook, K. L. Marino, and R. B. Cooper		8. Performing Organization Report No. EA-80-U-099
9. Performing Organization Name and Address Eclectech Associates, Incorporated North Stonington Professional Center North Stonington, CT 06359		10. Work Unit No. (TRAIS)
		11. Contract or Grant No. DOT-CG 944467-A
12. Sponsoring Agency Name and Address Department of Transportation U. S. Coast Guard (DMT-1/54) Office of Research and Development Washington, D. C. 20590		13. Type of Report and Period Covered Final Report
		14. Sponsoring Agency Code

15. Supplementary Notes The U. S. Coast Guard Project Manager and Monitor were Dr. John S. Gardenier and LTJG Paul T. Neiswander, respectively. Advice and guidance were provided by CAPT James T. Montonye, LCDR Leo Vaske and Mr. David A. Walden.

16. Abstract

The study used a ship's bridge simulator to investigate safety of navigation, the effect of navigation displays, and the effect of bridge personnel organization during low visibility approaches of a VLCC to a deepwater port complex. Experienced VLCC masters and mates, some team trained and team organized, performed over 90 simulated approaches to the Louisiana Offshore Oil Port (LOOP) using either radar, radar with added racons in the area an automatic radar plotting aid (ARPA), or an ARPA displaying fairway boundary lines. Three scenarios were examined: a landfall approach, coastwise approach, approach to pick up the mooring master, and a dead reckoning approach with degraded position information. Strategies which were chosen by the masters in their approaches are described in light of their effect on deepwater port safety. Conclusions derived from descriptive and statistical evidence of performance led to recommendations for relocating the mooring master pickup point, providing an anchorage for use by masters, and the placement and implementation of racons within the deepwater port area. Other recommendations advocate the use of special bridge procedures and navigation systems during port approaches, and further research into the effect of traffic separation or advisory schemes on deepwater port safety. Findings suggest that while approaches of VLCCs to an offshore deepwater port under conditions similar to those simulated are not deceptively difficult or inherently unsafe, there are opportunities to mitigate the potential for hazardous navigation and shiphandling problems.

17. Key Words Louisiana Offshore Oil Port (LOOP), port design, oil port, oil terminal, deepwater port, offshore port, inshore port, Gulf of Mexico port, port approach, port navigation, port safety, navigation hazard, (Cont'd)	18. Distribution Statement Document is available to the public through the National Technical Information Service Springfield, VA 22161		
19. Security Classif. (of this report) UNCLASSIFIED	20. Security Classif. (of this page) UNCLASSIFIED	21. No. of Pages 188	22. Price

Form DOT F 1700.7 (8-72) Reproduction of completed page authorized

Availability
Statement

Fig. 5
Technical Report Documentation Page

intended for indexers, use the title given there.

> U.S. Coast Guard. *A Simulator Study of Deepwater Port Shiphandling and Navigation Problems in Poor Visibility* by R.C. Cook, K.L. Marino, and R.B. Cooper (CG-D-66-80). Final Rpt. Washington: Government Printing Office, 1981. (TD5.25/2:66-80).

US 2.1b If you are using a government document on microfiche, look at the cover and title pages of the appropriate frames of the microfiche. Do not rely on the microfiche header for the title, since this information is not always accurate or complete. You must inform your reader that the document is on microfiche, usually by including this in parentheses after the title.

> U.S. Agency for International Development. *Kitale Maize: The Limits of Success* (microfiche). Washington: Government Printing Office, 1980. (S18.52:2).

US 2.1c The title of a map can usually be found centered at its head or in a lower corner on the face of the map.

> U.S. Central Intelligence Agency. *South Africa* (map). Washington: Government Printing Office, 1979. (PrEx3.10/4:So8a).

US 2.1d If the map has no title, cite it as untitled or make up a working title which should be placed in brackets.

> U.S. National Park Service. [Campgrounds of Yosemite] (map). Washington: Government Printing Office, 1972. (I29.2:Y8).

US 2.1e The titles of Congressional hearings will usually be found on the cover/title page at the head (Fig. 6). You should indicate in the title element, without underlining, that this is a hearing; its date (or dates); and the serial number, if any.

> U.S. House. Committee on Energy and Commerce. *Disapproving the FTC Funeral Rule* Hearing, 4 May 1983 (Serial No. 98-18). Washington: Government Printing Office, 1983. (Y4.En2/3:98-18).

US 2.2   Subtitles

Sometimes there is a subtitle to a document which might

$\mathcal{Y} \mathcal{U} . \mathcal{E}_r \, 2/3 \; 98-18$

DISAPPROVING THE FTC FUNERAL RULE ——— Title

HEARING

BEFORE THE

SUBCOMMITTEE ON
COMMERCE, TRANSPORTATION, AND TOURISM

OF THE

COMMITTEE ON ENERGY AND COMMERCE
HOUSE OF REPRESENTATIVES

NINETY-EIGHTH CONGRESS

FIRST SESSION

ON

H. CON. RES. 70

A CONCURRENT RESOLUTION DISAPPROVING A RULE SUBMITTED BY
THE FEDERAL TRADE COMMISSION RELATING TO FUNERAL
INDUSTRY PRACTICES

MAY 4, 1983 ————————————————— Date of Hearing

Serial No. 98-18

Printed for the use of the Committee on Energy and Commerce

U.S. GOVERNMENT PRINTING OFFICE

21-620 O   WASHINGTON : 1983

Fig. 6
U.S. Congressional Hearing: Title Page

distinguish a generic title or differentiate similar titles. Using
the subtitle may also help explain to your reader the relevance
of this title to your research. As a general rule separate the subtitle from the main title with a colon. If the title page of the
document uses some other punctuation, you may elect to use
that instead.

> U.S. National Institutes of Health. *Living with Asthma:*
> *Manual for Teaching Children the Self-management of*
> *Asthma* by Thomas L. Creer, Mary Backiel, and
> Patrick Leung. Draft. Washington: Government
> Printing Office, 1983. (HE20.3008:As8/draft).

US 2.3   Title Length

One of the outstanding characteristics of many government
documents is an excessively long title (e.g., *Statement of Edward*
C. Schmults Deputy Attorney General Department of Justice Before the
Subcommittee on Administrative Law and Governmental Relations Com-
mittee on the Judiciary House of Representatives Concerning Legislative
Veto on July 18, 1983). You need not cite the complete title; give
a sufficient portion of it so that your reader will be able to
distinguish the item from similar documents and be able to
locate it. To shorten a title, use ellipses (...) for any words
omitted. You can omit any number of words provided the citation makes sense and can still be located, but never omit the
initial four words of a title.

> U.S. Department of Justice. *Statement of Edward C.*
> *Schmults Deputy Attorney General ... Before the ...*
> *Committee on the Judiciary House ... Concerning*
> *Legislative Veto ....* Washington: Government
> Printing Office, 1983. (J1.2:Sch5).

US 2.4   Language of Title

If a federal document you are citing is written in a language
other than English, you should not translate the title, but cite it
as given.

> U.S. National Institutes of Health. *En Busca de Buena*
> *Salud Fumar: Este es el Mejor Momento para Dejarlo.*
> Bethesda, Md.: NIH, 1982.

US 2.5   Date in Title

If the title includes a date as a part of the title, include the date, even though it may seem to be repeating the date of publication.

> U.S. Department of the Treasury. *Daily Treasury State-*
> *ment, February 22, 1984.* Washington: Government
> Printing Office, 1984.

US 2.5a Occasionally documents are published and distributed long after their date of origin. The imprint and title dates will alert your reader to this fact.

> *Foreign Relations of the United States: The Conferences at*
> *Washington, 1941-42, and Casablanca, 1943.* Washing-
> ton: Government Printing Office, 1968.

US 2.5b For Congressional hearings there may be a date in the title. If there is, take it exactly as given and underline (italicize) it.

> U.S. House. Committee on Foreign Affairs. *U.S.*
> *Policy Toward Iran, January 1979* Hearing, 17 Jan.
> 1979. Washington: Government Printing Office,
> 1979. (Y4.F76/1:Ir1/979).

US 2.5c The actual date of a hearing is not usually included in the official title (Fig. 6). It should be given in the citation after the title, but it should not be underlined (italicized).

> U.S. House. Committee on Energy and Commerce.
> *Disapproving the FTC Funeral Rule* Hearing, 4 May
> 1983 (Serial No. 98-18). Washington: Government
> Printing Office, 1983. (Y4.En2/3:98-18).

US 2.5d For symposia and conference proceedings give the place and date of the meeting, but do not underline them.

> U.S. Department of Energy. Technical Information
> Center. *Energy and Environmental Stress in Aquatic*
> *Systems* Symposium, Augusta, Ga., 2-4 Nov. 1977
> (CONF-771114). Washington: DOE, 1978. (Sym-
> posium Series 48). (E1.10:771114; also available
> NTIS CONF-771114).

US 2.6 **Personal Authors**

When a personal author is named in a government document, credit should be given in the citation. Place the name (or names) in normal order after the title and state the author's role (e.g., "by," "edited by"). Personal authors are those who: write, compile, edit, prepare, draw, create, etc. Personal authors are *not* those who: direct, supervise, order, or administer.

> U.S. Energy Information Administration. *Railroad Deregulation: Impact on Coal* by Ercan Tukenmez (DOE/EIA-0399). Washington: Government Printing Office, 1983. (E3.2:R13).

US 2.6a   If more than three authors are mentioned, name only the first and include the others in "et al." or "and others."

> U.S. Defense Nuclear Agency. *Operation Greenhouse– 1951* edited by L. Berkhouse et al. (DNA 6034F). Washington: Department of Defense, 1983.

US 2.7   Contractors as Authors

Sometimes an agency will contract with a private company to produce a document (see also US 8.28a and e). In such a case, give credit to the contracting company, as though it were an individual.

> U.S. Department of Housing and Urban Development. *Rehabilitation Guidelines 1982: 10 Guidelines on the Rehabilitation of Walls, Windows, and Roofs* prepared by National Institute of Building Sciences. Washington: Government Printing Office, 1983. (HH1.6/3:R26/8/982).

US 2.8   Agency Numbering Systems

Some documents have printed on the cover and/or title page a combination of numbers and letters called "agency report numbers." These numbers should be included in the citation for several reasons:

1) they are unique to each document;
2) many libraries use these numbers as part of the call number;
3) some indexes provide access by these numbers.

These numbers frequently appear in the upper right- or left-hand corner of a title page (Fig. 7). If your document pro-

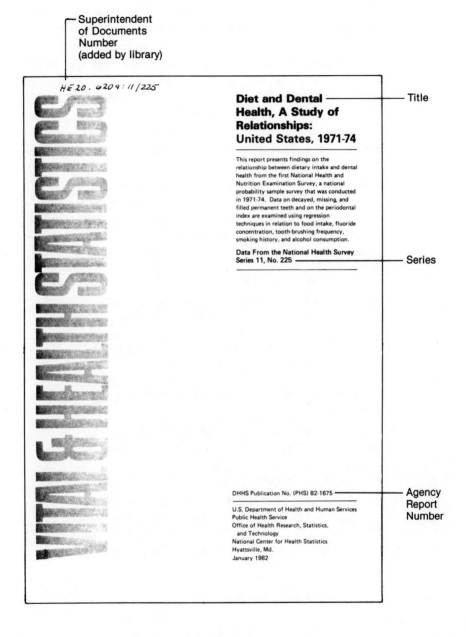

Superintendent
of Documents
Number
(added by library)

HE 20. 6209 : 11 /225

VITAL & HEALTH STATISTICS

**Diet and Dental ———— Title
Health, A Study of
Relationships:
United States, 1971-74**

This report presents findings on the
relationship between dietary intake and dental
health from the first National Health and
Nutrition Examination Survey, a national
probability sample survey that was conducted
in 1971-74. Data on decayed, missing, and
filled permanent teeth and on the periodontal
index are examined using regression
techniques in relation to food intake, fluoride
concentration, tooth-brushing frequency,
smoking history, and alcohol consumption.

**Data From the National Health Survey
Series 11, No. 225 ————— Series**

DHHS Publication No. (PHS) 82-1675 ———— Agency
Report
U.S. Department of Health and Human Services   Number
Public Health Service
Office of Health Research, Statistics,
  and Technology
National Center for Health Statistics
Hyattsville, Md.
January 1982

Fig. 7
Technical Report: Title Page

vides a "Bibliographic Data Sheet" or "Technical Report Documentation Page" (Fig. 5), the report number will be provided in a box labeled "report/accession number."

Do not confuse an agency report number with the classification number added by a library (Fig. 7). Do not confuse an agency report number with a contract or grant number. Grant/ contract numbers are not unique to a document, but are instead applied to every document which is a product of that contract or grant. Grant/contract numbers are usually indicated on the document by "Grant No. xxx" or "Contract No. xxx."

Agency report numbers should be placed in parentheses immediately after the title/personal author statement. These report numbers should be taken exactly as they appear on the document.

CONGRESSIONAL HEARING NUMBER

U.S. Senate. Committee on Banking, Housing, and Urban Affairs. *Gold and Silver Coinage Proposals* Hearing, 15 Apr. 1983 (S.Hrg.98-113). Washington: Government Printing Office, 1983. (Y4.B22/3: S.Hrg.98-113).

CONGRESSIONAL REPORT NUMBER

U.S. Senate. *Comprehensive Forfeiture Act of 1983, Report ... on S. 948* (S.Rpt.98-224). Washington: Government Printing Office, 1983. (Y1.1/5:98-224).

PUBLICATION NUMBER

U.S. National Center for Health Statistics. *Diet and Dental Health, A Study of Relationships: United States, 1971-74* (DHHS Pub. No. PHS 82-1675). Washington: Government Printing Office, 1982. (Vital and Health Statistics Series 11: Data from the National Health Survey No. 225). (HE20.6209: 11/225).

REPORT NUMBER

U.S. National Bureau of Standards. *Standard References in Selected Building Codes* by Bertram M. Vogel (NBSIR 76-1140). Washington, 1976.

US 2.9   Medium

The traditional medium of government documents has been "ink on paper:" books, periodicals, maps, posters. New technologies have introduced new media — microforms, computer tapes, slides, motion pictures, and audio or video tapes. The reasons for indicating the medium in a bibliographic citation are:

1) media other than books and periodicals may require special housing and may be placed in separate locations in libraries;
2) media other than "ink on paper" may require special equipment for use;
3) media other than "ink on paper" may be indexed only in special resources.

You should name the medium for audio or video tapes, audio-visual material, computer tapes, film strips, maps, microforms, and slides. Medium goes in parentheses after the title, personal author, and report number.

CASSETTE

U.S. Department of Labor. Women's Bureau. *Legal Rights of Women Workers* (audio-cassette). Washington, 1976.

COMPUTER TAPE (see also US 8.33)

U.S. Rural Electrification Administration. *Annual Statistical Report of the REA Power Supply Borrowers* (machine-readable data file). Washington: REA, 1973. (NTIS PB 238 401).

MAP

U.S. Central Intelligence Agency. *Major Shipping Routes of the World* (map). Washington: Government Printing Office, 1978.

MICROFICHE

U.S. Bureau of Outdoor Recreation. *National Urban Recreation Study: Dallas/Fort Worth* (microfiche). Washington: Government Printing Office, 1977. (I66.24:D16).

US 2.9a You need not indicate the medium when you include the information in a note (see US 6).

> U.S. Senate. *History of the Committee on Finance* (S.Doc.95-27). Washington: Government Printing Office, 1977. (1977 CIS microfiche S360-1).

US 3 EDITION

Sometimes a document will be revised and published a number of times with differing content. Examples of this would be the issuance of an environmental impact statement in draft and final form, or the second edition of the Surgeon General's report on *Smoking and Health*. Since the content may differ, you must inform your reader.

US 3.1 Edition Statement

Include the edition after the title data.

> U.S. Office of Personnel Management. *Resource Allocation Plan Model for Special Emphasis Program Managers* (OAEP-10). Ltd. ed. Washington: Government Printing Office, 1983. (PM1.2:R31).

US 3.1a If the edition is already indicated by the title, you need not repeat it.

> U.S. Forest Service. *Draft Environmental Impact Statement Rio Grande National Forest.* Washington: Government Printing Office, 1983. (A13.92/2:R47).

US 3.1b If the edition is indicated in the report number, you need not repeat it.

> U.S. Department of Housing and Urban Development. *Public Housing Development Handbook* (HUD Handbook 7417.1, Rev.1). Washington: Government Printing Office, 1980. (HH1.6/6:7417.1).

US 3.2 Map Edition

A map can also be reissued with changes and be known as "photorevised." Be sure to indicate that to your reader if you have such an item.

U.S. Geological Survey. *Julian, Pa.* (map). Photorevised 1971. Washington: USGS, 1961. (1:2500).

US 4   IMPRINT

"Imprint" is a bibliographic term for the facts of publication,
including place of publication, publisher, and date. The rationale for including these data is to distinguish among titles and to
alert the reader to a potential source for an item.

US 4.1   Place of Publication

The place of publication can usually be found on the front or
the back of the title page. Sometimes it will be found on the
bottom of the last page of the text. If the item is available from
or printed by GPO, the place is assumed to be Washington,
D.C.

> U.S. Library of Congress. *Wilbur & Orville Wright:*
> *Pictorial Materials* by Arthur G. Renstrom. Washing-
> ton: Government Printing Office, 1982. (LC1.6/4:
> W93).

US 4.1a   Should this not be the case, look for the mailing address on the
back of the document, in a preface, or in a letter of transmittal.

> U.S. Forest Service. *Estimating Soil Erosion Using an*
> *Erosion Bridge* by Darlene G. Blaney and Gordon E.
> Warrington (WSDG-TP-00008). Fort Collins,
> Colo., 1983.

US 4.1b   If you cannot make a reasonable guess as to the place of publication, use n.p. (no place).

> U.S. Federal Insurance Administration. *In the Event of*
> *a Flood.* n.p., 1983.

US 4.2   Publisher

Publishing practices in the federal government are not quite the
same as those in the commercial sector. Strictly speaking,
agencies are the publishers since they alone have editorial control. However, citing the GPO, NTIS, or ERIC (i.e. the major
printers/distributors) will lead your reader more quickly to the
relevant indexes and to a source for purchase (see US 8.28).

The publisher can usually be found on the front or the back of the title page or on the bottom of the last page of text. If the GPO is named anywhere on the document as printer, publisher, or sales agent, assume that it is the publisher.

> U.S. Department of Justice. Bureau of Justice Statistics. *A Style Manual for Machine Readable Data Files and Their Documentation* by Richard C. Roistacher (SD-T-3; NCJ62766). Washington: Government Printing Office, 1980. (J29.9:SD-T-3).

US 4.2a Sometimes the agencies themselves are the source of the document. This may be indicated on a mailing label, in a letter of transmittal, or on a bibliographic data sheet. In such cases, the agency can be assumed to be the publisher. If the name has already been given in full as the author, you may abbreviate.

> U.S. Small Business Administration. *Women's Handbook: How SBA Can Help You Go Into Business*. Fort Worth, Tex.: SBA, 1983.

US 4.2b If you cannot determine a publisher, simply give the place and date of publication.

> U.S. Forest Service. *Estimating Soil Erosion Using an Erosion Bridge* by Darlene G. Blaney and Gordon E. Warrington (WSDG-TP-00008). Fort Collins, Colo., 1983.

US 4.3   Date of Publication

The date of publication is essential for later location and verification of an item since none of the standard indexes is totally cumulative. The date of publication can be found in a number of places: title page, front or back; embedded in a report number; in a preface or a letter of transmittal; or at the bottom of the last page.

> U.S. Department of State. *Soviet Active Measures, September 1983*. Washington: Government Printing Office, 1983. (Special Report No. 110). (S1.129:110).

US 4.3a If the document has no printed date, but does have a library date-stamp, use that date in brackets with "by." This will tell your reader that the document would have been published by that date.

> U.S. Department of Defense. *Radar Training Manual* (DATM 90-2-AX). Washington: DOD, [by 1975].

US 4.3b If you cannot find a date, use n.d. (no date).

> U.S. Forest Service. Pacific Northwest Region. *Forests for the Future: Growing New Forests in the Pacific Northwest.* n.p., n.d. (6 leaflets).

US 5 **SERIES**

A series is a group of publications under one group title with distinct titles for individual works. Individual titles may or may not be numbered. It is a good idea to include series in a citation because:

1) it is often a shortcut in locating the document;
2) if a bibliographic record (index, card catalog, etc.) does not distinguish individual titles in series, the series name may be the *only* way of locating it.

US 5.1 **Series Name and Number**

The full series name and the number of the document should come in parentheses after the imprint data (Fig. 7).

> U.S. Department of State. *United States Foreign Policy 1972: A Report of the Secretary of State.* Washington: Government Printing Office, 1973. (General Foreign Policy Series 274). (S1.71:274).

US 5.1a If a series number is given in the report number, you need not repeat the report number in the series statement.

> U.S. Environmental Protection Agency. *Bioflocculation and the Accumulation of Chemicals by Floc-Forming Organisms* by Patrick R. Dugan (EPA-600/2-75-032). Washington: Government Printing Office, 1975. (Environmental Protection Technology Series). (EP1.23/2:600/2-75-032).

US 5.2 **More Than One Series**

When citing a series within a series, you must give both series names.

> U.S. Bureau of the Census. *Voting and Registration in the Election of November 1982.* Washington: Government Printing Office, 1983. (Current Population Reports; P-20 Population Characteristics No. 383). (C3.186: P20/383).

US 6   NOTES

"Notes" is a catch-all category in which you can place significant information which does not fit in other segments of the citation. Anything included in notes should be in parentheses at the end of the citation. Depending upon the specific data, notes may or may not be required.

US 6.1   Required Notes

Required notes are those which would help your reader find *precisely* the same material you have in hand (e.g., a microform collection number; a serial set number; a Superintendent of Documents number, if available). Also required are indications about the publication which would affect the reader's ability to locate or use the information source (e.g., FOIA obtained documents, unpublished papers, mimeographed items, distribution data, looseleafs).

DISTRIBUTION DATA

> U.S. Air Force University. *Strategy for Defeat: The Luftwaffe 1933-1945* by Williamson Murray. Maxwell Air Force Base, Ala.: Air University Press, 1983. (Distributed by the Government Printing Office; D301.2:St7).

LOOSELEAF FORMAT

> "Federal Employees Required to File Financial Disclosure Reports" (FPM Letter 734-1; 4 Nov. 1982). In U.S. Office of Personnel Management. *Federal Personnel Manual.* Washington: Government Printing Office. (Looseleaf).

MICROFORM COLLECTION ENTRY NUMBERS

CIS Microfiche

> U.S. Senate. *History of the Committee on Finance*

(S.Doc.95-27). Washington: Government Printing
Office, 1977. (1977 CIS microfiche S360-1).

Government Printing Office Microfiche
U.S. House. 97th Congress, 1st Session. *H.R. 3, A*
Bill to Amend the Internal Revenue Code of 1954 . . . .
Washington: Government Printing Office, 1981.
(GPO microfiche 10, coordinate D4).

Readex
U.S. Department of Health, Education and Welfare.
Management by Objectives: Planning Where to Go and
How to Get There by T.H. Bell. n.p., 1974. (1974
Readex non-dep. microcard 01191).

MIMEOGRAPHED DOCUMENTS
(in-house documents)
U.S. Department of Education. *Investigation into Adoles-*
cent Promiscuity. n.p., 1977. (Mimeo).

SERIAL SET VOLUME NUMBERS
U.S. House. Select Committee on Small Business.
Organization and Operation of the Small Business Admin-
istration: A Report . . . Pursuant to H.Res. 46 . . .
(H.Rpt.87-2564). Washington: Government Print-
ing Office, 1963. (Serial Set 12440).

SUPERINTENDENT OF DOCUMENTS NUMBER
(if known)
U.S. Smithsonian Institution. *Through Looking to Learn-*
ing: The Museum Adventure edited by Thomas E.
Lowderbaugh. Washington: Smithsonian Institution
Press, 1983. (S1.2:M97/6).

US 6.2   Optional Notes

Optional notes are those which would help your reader determine the quality of the document (e.g., poster, pamphlet). Also
optional is information about language or the size of non-print
media (e.g., map scale or frame size).

LANGUAGE
U.S. Department of Education. *MANAd* by Elnora
Mapatis. Washington: Government Printing Office,
1983. (Recounted in Hualapai).

MAP SCALE

U.S. Geological Survey. *State College, Pa.* (map).
Photorevised 1971. Washington: USGS, 1962.
(1:2400).

PUBLICATION TYPE

U.S. National Park Service. *Moore's Creek.* Washington:
Government Printing Office, 1983 (I29.2:M78;
pamphlet and map).

US 7 CITING PARTS: ARTICLES, CHAPTERS, AND LOOSELEAFS

In citing a part of a publication (e.g., an article from a
periodical, a chapter from a book, an insert from a hearing)
you must use both the title of the part and the title of the whole.
If you cite only the article, the reader will not be able to locate
your source. If you cite only the source, the reader will not be
able to locate the particular part which you considered relevant
to your topic.

US 7.1 Periodicals

Periodicals (journals, magazines, newspapers, etc.) are publications issued with some frequency (more than once a year)
whose titles do not change from issue to issue and whose contents include a variety of articles, stories, columns, editorials,
notices, etc. Some examples are the *FBI Law Enforcement
Bulletin, EPA Journal, Federal Register,* and *Congressional Record.*
   A typical periodical citation includes the personal author
of the article, the article's title, title of the periodical, volume
and issue numbers, date, and pagination.

Gorsuch, Anne M. "The 1980's: A Decade of Chal-
lenge," *EPA Journal* 8:1(Jan.-Feb. 1982) pp. 5-9.
(EP1.67:8/1).

US 7.1a Note that in some of the following periodical citations the issuing agency was included as a note. In most libraries and for
most non-government periodicals you need to know only the
name of the periodical to find it. This is not always true for
government periodicals. Libraries which keep government
documents separate from the rest of their collection may also

keep government periodicals separate from other periodicals. Further, the standard catalogs of periodicals do not include all government periodicals. Including the name of the issuing agency in a note will help your reader locate an otherwise obscure title. This tells your readers to look in sources that list government periodicals.

> Cantor, Norman F. "Why Study the Middle Ages?" *Humanities* 3:3(June 1982) pp. 21-30. (Issued by the U.S. National Endowment for the Humanities; NF3.11:3/3).

US 7.1b If the article has more than one author, cite both; invert the name of the first author, so that the citation will file alphabetically in your bibliography. If there are more than three authors, cite the first one only and use "et al." or "and others" to cover the other authors (see US 2.6a).

> Greenburg, Martin A. and Ellen C. Wertleib. "The Police and the Elderly (Pt. II)," *FBI Law Enforcement Bulletin* 52:9(Sept. 1983) pp. 1-7. (J1.14/8: 52/9).

US 7.1c If no author is listed for the article, start your citation with the article's title and omit the author segment of the citation.

> "ABA Approves Model Rules of Professional Conduct," *The Third Branch: Bulletin of the Federal Court* 15:9(Sept. 1983) pp. 5, 8. (Publication of the Federal Judicial Center; Ju10.3/2:15/9).

US 7.2   Non-periodicals

Usually when you cite a work, other than a periodical article, you cite the whole work. There are cases, however, where you might want to cite only a part of a work — a single paper in a collection of conference papers, a single article in an encyclopedic kind of source, or a piece of evidence inserted in a Congressional hearing. When to cite the whole work and when to cite only a part will depend on the purposes of your bibliography. How to cite a part will depend on the nature of the whole.

A citation to a part of any non-periodical publication is like the citation to the whole publication except that it is preceded by the part's author/title and by the range of pages, as appropriate.

CHAPTER IN A BOOK

Striner, Richard. "Washington Present: Our Nation's Capitol Today," pp. 54-135. In U.S. Capitol Historical Society. *Washington Past and Present.* Washington: U.S. Capitol Historical Society, 1983.

CHAPTER IN AN ENCYCLOPEDIC SOURCE

"Engineers," pp. 57-66. In U.S. Bureau of Labor Statistics. *Occupational Outlook Handbook.* 1982-83 ed. Washington: Government Printing Office, 1982. (BLS Bulletin 2200).

MICROFICHE INSERTED IN PAPER TEXT

U.S. National Oceanic and Atmospheric Administration. "Determination of Petroleum Components in Samples from the Metula Oil Spill" by J.S. Warner (NOAA DR ERL MESA 4; microfiche). Boulder, Colo.: NOAA, 1976. In U.S. National Oceanic and Atmospheric Administration. *The Metula Oil Spill* by Charles G. Gunnerson and George Peter. Washington: Government Printing Office, 1976. (C55.602:M56).

PAPER IN CONFERENCE PROCEEDINGS

Takahashi, H. "Fission Reaction in High Energy Proton Cascade," pp. 133-145. In U.S. Department of Energy. Brookhaven National Laboratory. *Symposium on Neutron Cross-Sections* Brookhaven National Laboratory, 12-14 May 1980 (BNL-NCS-51245; DOE/NDC-21/L). Washington: Government Printing Office, 1980. (E1.28:BNL-NCS-51245; also available NTIS).

PAPER INSERTED IN A CONGRESSIONAL HEARING

Robins and Assoc. "Comparative Analysis of Sediment Pond Design Requirements: Interim Versus Final Federal Regulations (June 13, 1979)," pp. 89-110. In U.S. Senate. Committee on Energy and Natural Resources. *Oversight — The Surface Mining*

Control and Reclamation Act of 1977 Hearings, 19, 21
June 1979. Washington: Government Printing
Office, 1979. (Y4.En2:96-44).

US 7.3   Looseleafs

Some government publications come in looseleaf format so that
they can be easily updated. These are usually the procedural
documents of the government bureaucracy — manuals, guide-
lines, regulations, standards, etc. They are often massive, and
their internal organization may be complicated.

In citing these publications, you will usually be citing a
specific part rather than the whole. The information to include
will depend on the organization of the looseleaf and will usually
be the name of the part, the internal filing numbers, and a
date. The date of the part to which you are referring is important, since it is entirely possible that the part you are citing will
be superseded later by an amendment with the same number
and name. The date will usually be printed at the top or bottom of each page.

Information about the volume or set should include: issuing agency, title, agency report number (if any), place,
publisher, series number (if any), and "looseleaf" in a note.
You will note that the date of the main volume is omitted. If
you can find an edition date for the whole publication, you may
include it. However, it will be simply the date for the reprinted
whole edition and will likely have changes of later dates filed in.

Looseleafs may be organized in many ways — by part
number, by page number, or by some other system especially
adapted to the contents of the looseleaf. You must look at the
publication and give the information which best locates the part
you are citing.

LOOSELEAF ORGANIZED
BY SECTION NUMBER
"Telegraphic Bids" (Sect. 1-2.202-2 FPR Amendment
229; Mar. 1983). In U.S. General Services Administration. *Federal Procurement Regulations.* 2nd ed.;
reprinted 1981. Washington: Government Printing
Office. (Looseleaf; GS1.6/5:964/rep.5).

LOOSELEAF ORGANIZED
BY PAGE NUMBER

"Performance Funding System" (pp. 1-10; Feb. 1977).
In U.S. Department of Housing and Urban Devel-
opment. *Performance Funding System Handbook* (HUD
Handbook 7475.13). Washington: HUD.
(Looseleaf; HH1.6/6:7475.13).

LOOSELEAF ORGANIZED
BY METHOD NUMBER

"Sampling for Inspection and Testing" (Method 1022;
1 Feb. 1980). In U.S. General Services Administra-
tion. *Paint, Varnish, Lacquer and Related Materials:
Methods for Sampling and Testing.* Washington:
Government Printing Office. (Federal Test Method
Standard Number 141B). (Looseleaf; GS2.8/7:141B).

US 8   SPECIAL CASES

Certain federal titles and some types of U.S. government documents are so frequently cited or present such unique problems
that they require special rules. For your convenience they are
discussed separately in this section. Many of these titles are so
well-known or appear in so many editions and formats that you
can leave it to your reader to find a source. For this reason it is
not necessary to include all citation elements.

US 8.1   Constitution

The U.S. Constitution can be found in many places. If citing
the whole Constitution, give your source and its date. Since the
Constitution has been amended over time, it may be important
for the reader to know which version is being cited.

> *The Constitution of the United States of America: Analysis and
> Interpretation* (S.Doc.92-82). Washington: Govern-
> ment Printing Office, 1973. (Serial Set 12980-7).

US 8.1a

It is more likely that you will cite a part of the Constitution —
an article, a section, or an amendment. In this case, your
source is not so important since numerous sources will contain
precisely that part.

> U.S. Constitution. Art. I, Sect. 1.

US 8.2   Government Manual

The *U.S. Government Manual* is a product of the General Services Administration. However, since this title is a standard reference work, it is not necessary to include the name of the issuing agency. Simple citation to the item itself will suffice.

> *The United States Government Manual 1983/84.* Washington: Government Printing Office, 1983.

US 8.3   Statutes at Large

To cite a public law found in the *Statutes at Large,* include the name of the law, its public law number (P.L.), date of passage, volume, and page numbers. The name of the law can usually be located in the first paragraph of the text or in the annotations on the side of the page (Fig. 8).

> "Omnibus Budget Reconciliation Act of 1981" (PL 97-35, 13 Aug. 1981), *United States Statutes at Large* 95, pp. 357-933.

US 8.3a

After passage, laws are first printed as pamphlets known as "slip laws." These can be cited by the name of the law, public law number, and date of passage.

> "Omnibus Budget Reconciliation Act of 1981" (PL 97-35, 13 Aug. 1981).

US 8.4   U.S. Code (USC)

To cite a section of the *U.S. Code* give the name of the section, *U.S. Code,* the title and part number, and the year of the edition. Since the *U.S. Code* is constantly changing, the year of the edition is crucial.

> "Community Mental Health Center," *U.S. Code,* Title 42, Pts. 2689 et seq. 1976 ed.

US 8.4a

The *U.S. Code* is updated annually by supplements for five years. The supplements are then incorporated into a new edition. When citing a section which appears in a supplement, give the original edition and the supplement number and its year.

> "Vocational Rehabilitation Services," *U.S. Code,*

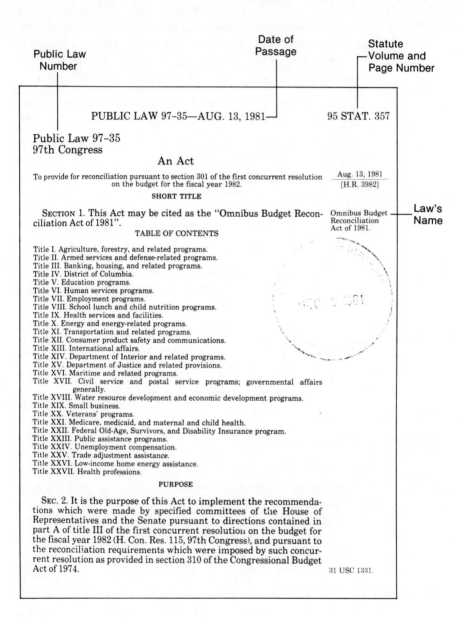

Public Law
Number

Date of
Passage

Statute
Volume and
Page Number

PUBLIC LAW 97-35—AUG. 13, 1981—   95 STAT. 357

Public Law 97-35
97th Congress

An Act

To provide for reconciliation pursuant to section 301 of the first concurrent resolution on the budget for the fiscal year 1982.

Aug. 13, 1981
[H.R. 3982]

SHORT TITLE

SECTION 1. This Act may be cited as the "Omnibus Budget Reconciliation Act of 1981".

Omnibus Budget
Reconciliation
Act of 1981.

Law's
Name

TABLE OF CONTENTS

PURPOSE

SEC. 2. It is the purpose of this Act to implement the recommendations which were made by specified committees of the House of Representatives and the Senate pursuant to directions contained in part A of title III of the first concurrent resolution on the budget for the fiscal year 1982 (H. Con. Res. 115, 97th Congress), and pursuant to the reconciliation requirements which were imposed by such concurrent resolution as provided in section 310 of the Congressional Budget Act of 1974.

31 USC 1331.

Fig. 8

First Page of a Law

Title 29, Pts. 720 et seq. 1976 ed. Supp. V, 1981.

US 8.5 Federal Register

To cite the *Federal Register* give the name of the section, any identifying agency report numbers, *Federal Register,* volume, issue, date, and pagination. You should also include as part of the section name an indication of what action is represented (e.g., final rule, proposed rule to amend . . ., executive order, proclamation).

> "Establishment of Sonoma County Green Valley
> Viticultural Area, Final Rule" (T.D. ATF-161),
> *Federal Register* 48:125(21 Nov. 1983) p. 52577.

US 8.6 Code of Federal Regulations (CFR)

To cite the *Code of Federal Regulations* give the name of the section, *Code of Federal Regulations,* title and part numbers, and edition. Since the CFR is reissued annually and substantial regulatory changes may be enacted, inclusion of the edition statement is essential.

> "Confidentiality of Alcohol and Drug Abuse Patient
> Records," *Code of Federal Regulations* Title 42, Pt. 2.
> 1982 ed.

US 8.7 U.S. Reports

Give the full name of the case (plaintiff v. defendant), *U.S. Reports,* volume, date of the decision, and page numbers.

> Brown v. the Board of Education of Topeka, Shawnee
> County, Kansas, *U.S. Reports* 347(17 May 1954)
> pp. 483-500.

US 8.8 Congressional Record

In citing the bound edition of the *Congressional Record* it is advisable to name the speaker, the title of the section, the volume number and part number of the *Record,* the date, and the pages cited. You need not include the Congress and session numbers since such information is superfluous. By giving the date of publication and volume/part number you have provided a check for your reader should a piece of data be inaccurately transposed. You should also identify the home state of the speaker. This may not seem important with unusual or famous names, but with common names such as Anderson or Smith, it can serve to distinguish two speakers for your reader.

> Rep. Anderson (Cal.). "Legislation for the Care of
> Vietnamese Refugees," *Congressional Record* 121, Pt.
> 10(25 Apr. 1975) pp. 12-52.

US 8.8a For a general debate with several speakers, simply give the name of the section.

> "Religion and Schools," *Congressional Record* 20,
> Pt. 1(21 Dec. 1888) pp. 433-434.

US 8.8b In citing the daily edition of the *Congressional Record,* be sure to indicate that fact. The pagination in the daily edition changes once the item is included in a bound volume. Because of these changes, it is necessary to give sufficient information as to speaker, subject, date, etc. so that your reader could later locate the citation in the bound volumes.

> Sens. Hawkins (Fla.), Grassley (Ia.) and Packwood
> (Ore.). "Radio Marti," *Congressional Record* (12
> Sept. 1983). Daily ed. S11970-11981.

US 8.9 **Congressional Globe, Register of Debates,**
and Annals of Congress

The *Congressional Globe,* the *Register,* and the *Annals* are cited much like the *Congressional Record* (US 8.8), except that since there are no consistent volume numbers, the number of the Congress; the session number; and the part, if applicable, must be given. If there is no title, a descriptive statement can be used in its place.

ANNALS OF CONGRESS

> "Trial of Samuel Chase," *Annals of Congress* 8th Con-
> gress, 2nd Session (1804-1805) pp. 81-676.

CONGRESSIONAL GLOBE

> Sen. Polk (Mo.). Speech on the State of the Union,
> *Congressional Globe* 36th Congress, 2nd Session (14
> Jan. 1861) Pt. 1, pp. 355-360.

CONGRESSIONAL GLOBE, APPENDIX

Sen. Smith (Conn.). "Claims for French Spoliations," *Congressional Globe, Appendix* 31st Congress, 2nd Session (16 Jan. 1851) pp. 115-126.

REGISTER OF DEBATES

"Gratitude to Lafayette," *Register of Debates* 18th Congress, 2nd Session (21 Dec. 1824) pp. 28-35.

US 8.10   Journals of the Continental Congress

There have been many editions of the *Journals.* How you cite them will depend upon the organization of the edition used. In every case the imprint (place, publisher, date) should be given. The Library of Congress edition is the most complete and most widely available. Its volumes are numbered consecutively; therefore, the volume number will locate an item precisely. However, it is a good idea to include the date of the Continental Congress in parentheses for your reader's convenience.

THE WHOLE SET

U.S. Library of Congress. *Journals of the Continental Congress 1774-1789.* Washington: Government Printing Office, 1904.

INDIVIDUAL VOLUME

U.S. Library of Congress. *Journals of the Continental Congress 1774-1789,* Vol. I(1774). Washington: Government Printing Office, 1904.

SINGLE ENTRY OR DOCUMENT WITHIN A VOLUME

"Address to the People of Great Britain," pp. 81-90. In U.S. Library of Congress. *Journals of the Continental Congress 1774-1789,* Vol. I(1774). Washington: Government Printing Office, 1904.

US 8.11   House (or Senate) Journal

Since titles are not usually given to sections of the *Journals,* just give the speaker, state, and subject. Then include Congress, session, date, and page numbers.

Albert, Carl (Okla.). Remarks, *Journal of the House of*

Representatives 94th Congress, 1st Session (14 Jan. 1975) pp. 2-4.

US 8.12   Congressional Directory

The *Congressional Directory* is published once every Congress and is updated by a paper supplement. Since the title implies the issuing agency, it is not necessary to repeat the agency.

> *Congressional Directory, 1983-84.* 98th Congress. Washington: Government Printing Office, 1983.

US 8.13   Bills

For bills, resolutions, acts, and star prints, the issuing agency is either "U.S. Senate" or "U.S. House," with no committee designation. These publications are issued by the entire Congressional chamber, not by a committee. You must also include the Congress and session number in the issuing agency statement (see US 1.3f).

US 8.13a The number of a bill or resolution is its most descriptive feature and should be used with the title. You may shorten the title from the text, if necessary (Fig. 9).

> U.S. House. 96th Congress, 1st Session. *H.R. 2, A Bill To Require Authorization for Budget Authority . . . .* Washington: Government Printing Office, 1979.

US 8.13b The legislative process may result in many amended versions of a bill or resolution, if a bill sees any action. Include either "Act" or "Star Print," as applicable, in the edition statement. An act is indicated in the bill's title. A star print is indicated by a small star on the lower left corner of the title page (Fig. 9).

> U.S. Senate. 97th Congress, 1st Session. *S. Res. 148, Resolution . . . for a Moratorium . . . on the Commercial Killing of Whales.* Star Print. Washington: Government Printing Office, 1982.

US 8.13c Since 1979 the GPO has been distributing bills and resolutions on microfiche; few institutions retained back files of these bills in paper form. Therefore, it is extremely likely that you will be citing, and your reader will be looking for, the microfiche edi-

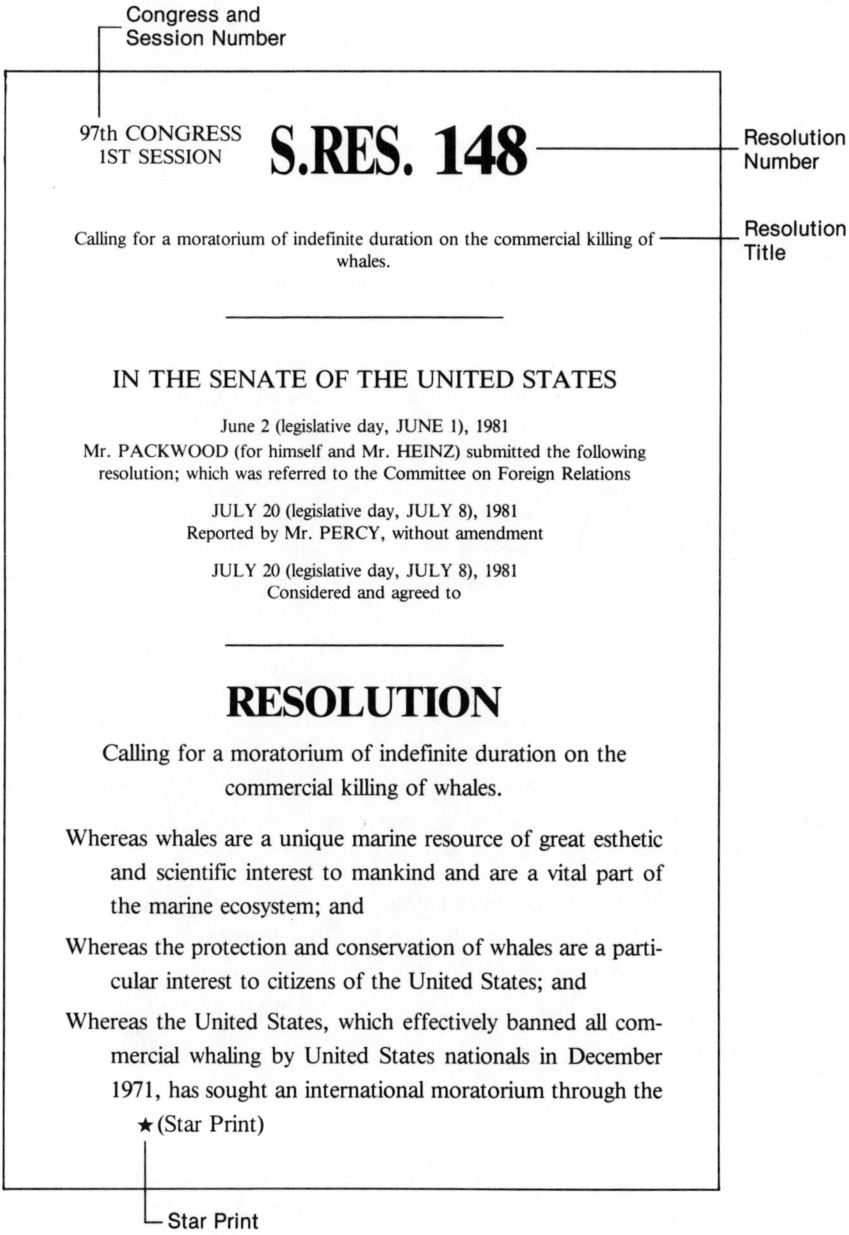

Congress and
Session Number

97th CONGRESS
1ST SESSION **S.RES. 148** Resolution Number

Calling for a moratorium of indefinite duration on the commercial killing of whales. Resolution Title

---

IN THE SENATE OF THE UNITED STATES

June 2 (legislative day, JUNE 1), 1981
Mr. PACKWOOD (for himself and Mr. HEINZ) submitted the following
resolution; which was referred to the Committee on Foreign Relations

JULY 20 (legislative day, JULY 8), 1981
Reported by Mr. PERCY, without amendment

JULY 20 (legislative day, JULY 8), 1981
Considered and agreed to

RESOLUTION

Calling for a moratorium of indefinite duration on the
commercial killing of whales.

Whereas whales are a unique marine resource of great esthetic
and scientific interest to mankind and are a vital part of
the marine ecosystem; and

Whereas the protection and conservation of whales are a particular interest to citizens of the United States; and

Whereas the United States, which effectively banned all commercial whaling by United States nationals in December
1971, has sought an international moratorium through the

★ (Star Print)

Star Print

Fig. 9
U.S. Congressional Bill

tion. In order to facilitate location of the bill, you should include the fiche number and frame coordinates as a note.

> U.S. House. 98th Congress, 1st Session. *H.R. 1791, A Bill To Amend the Social Security Act* . . . . Washington: Government Printing Office, 1983. (GPO microfiche 101, coordinate E4).

US 8.13d It is not unusual for a bill to be reprinted in its entirety in a hearing, report, or in the *Congressional Record.* If that is your text, cite it as part of the larger source.

> U.S. Senate. 94th Congress, 1st Session. "S.Res. 55, To Establish Legislative Review Subcommittees," *Congressional Record* 121, Pt. 2(3 Feb. 1975) p. 2078.

US 8.14   Serial Set

The U.S. Serial Set is the official compilation of Congressional reports and documents. At one time nearly all government publications were issued as Congressional documents in the Serial Set. Thus, they all have a Congressional number (e.g., 42nd Congress, House Miscellaneous Doc. 242). The bound volumes are numbered consecutively from 1817 onward.

To cite material in the Serial Set you should give the Congress, session, title, and number (e.g., 58-2, House Report 21). If available also give imprint data. Inclusion of the Serial Set number is recommended and should be placed in a note.

> U.S. Senate. 50th Congress, 2nd Session. *Report on Indian Traderships* (S.Rpt.2707). Washington: Government Printing Office, 1899. (Serial Set 2623).

US 8.15   American State Papers

The *American State Papers* (ASP) is a compilation of the publications of the early Congresses, arranged in broad categories. With the Serial Set it forms the most complete collection available of Congressional reports and documents. Since the documents in ASP are *not* chronologically arranged, it is necessary to cite subject area, volume, report number, and page numbers.

> "Naval Register for 1832," *American State Papers: Naval*

Affairs, Vol. IV (Doc.461) pp. 48-63.

US 8.16 Foreign Relations of the United States

Foreign Relations of the United States, published since 1861, is a compilation of the diplomatic papers of the U.S. The set is arranged by year and within that year by volumes (and occasionally parts) which cover various geographic areas or policy issues. Due to classification and secrecy, these papers are not released for publication for many years; thus, the publication date will differ considerably from the year covered. Therefore, it is vital to your reader that you include both dates: one for locating and one for informational purposes.

> *Foreign Relations of the United States, 1949, Vol. VIII,*
> *Pt. 2: The Far East and Australia.* Washington:
> Government Printing Office, 1976.

US 8.16a To cite a single document within *Foreign Relations of the U.S.:*

> "The Secretary of State to the Embassy in Greece,"
> pp. 533-534. In *Foreign Relations of the United States,*
> *1951, Vol. V: The Near East and North Africa.*
> Washington: Government Printing Office, 1982.

US 8.16b Some volumes fall outside the annual series. These are compilations devoted to a single subject (Japan 1931-1941; Paris Peace Conference, 1919; etc). In citations of these documents the name comes before the date of a volume number in the title to distinguish them from the annual compilations.

> *Foreign Relations of the United States: The Conferences at*
> *Washington, 1941-42, and Casablanca, 1943.* Washington: Government Printing Office, 1968.

US 8.17 Treaties

U.S. treaties are published in two forms: as individual documents in the *Treaties and Other International Acts Series* (TIAS) and in *United States Treaties* (UST), the standard treaty compilation. In both they are arranged sequentially by TIAS number. You should cite the title, the parties, the date of signing, and the TIAS number. Other elements will depend on whether you are citing *TIAS* or *UST.*

Take the title from the first page of the treaty. Use the first form of agreement listed (e.g., treaty, convention, agreement), followed by a short title based on the subject matter. Since the U.S. is party to all treaties in these series, it is necessary to include only the other party in bilateral treaties and designate "multilateral" for multilateral treaties. Give the first and last dates of signing if there are more than one. Multilateral treaties may say "done at" rather than "signed." In any case use the date on the cover page of *TIAS*.

TIAS CITATION

"Convention on Atomic Energy," Sweden, signed
27 Jan., 23 Feb. 1981, *Treaties and Other International Acts Series 10099.*

UST CITATION

"General Agreement on Tariffs and Trade," done
10 Mar. 1955, Multilateral (TIAS 3437), *United States Treaties* 6, Pt. 5(1955) p. 5815.

US 8.18   Weekly Compilation of Presidential Documents

The *Weekly Compilation* can be cited like a typical periodical. The title should include the title of the article, nature of the document (e.g., speech, executive order, proclamation), and the date of the document.

"Veterans Day, 1976" (Proclamation 4458, 9 Sept. 1976), *Weekly Compilation of Presidential Documents* 12:37(13 Sept. 1976) pp. 1323-1324.

US 8.18a   If the nature of the document and its date are given in the title, they do not need to be repeated.

"The President's News Conference of October 19, 1983," *Weekly Compilation of Presidential Documents* 19:42(24 Oct. 1983) pp. 1465-1472.

US 8.19   Public Papers of the Presidents

The bound compilations of Presidential documents are arranged by President, year, and volume number (if there is more than one volume in the year). As in standard sources, the title should be first and then the President's name. Since there are other non-governmental editions available, it is necessary to include imprint data.

ALL THE VOLUMES OF A PRESIDENT

Public Papers of the Presidents of the United States: John F. Kennedy. Washington: Government Printing Office, 1962-1964.

A SINGLE VOLUME OF A PRESIDENT

Public Papers of the Presidents of the United States: John F. Kennedy, 1961. Washington: Government Printing Office, 1962.

A SINGLE DOCUMENT

"Inaugural Address" (20 Jan. 1961), pp. 1-3. In *Public Papers of the Presidents of the United States: John F. Kennedy, 1961.* Washington: Government Printing Office, 1962.

A NON-GOVERNMENT EDITION

The Public Papers and Addresses of Franklin D. Roosevelt. New York: Random House, 1938-1950.

US 8.20 Economic Report of the President

The Economic Report of the President appears in two editions each year: the Congressional and the executive branch version. The Congressional version will have a House document number.

CONGRESSIONAL VERSION

Economic Report of the President February 1983 (H.Doc.98-2). Washington: Government Printing Office, 1983.

EXECUTIVE BRANCH VERSION

Economic Report of the President February 1983. Washington: Government Printing Office, 1983.

US 8.21 Budget of the United States

The *Budget of the United States* appears in two editions: Congressional and executive branch. To differentiate between the two look for the Congressional numbering scheme on the document.

CONGRESSIONAL VERSION

Budget of the United States Fiscal Year 1984 (H.Doc.98-3). Washington: Government Printing Office, 1983.

EXECUTIVE BRANCH VERSION

Budget of the United States Fiscal Year 1984. Washington: Government Printing Office, 1983.

US 8.22   Census

The U.S. Census is extremely complex and may require varying pieces of information for any citation. The key is to include enough information so that your reader can locate a volume or part of the census.

You should always include the complete title and census year of the report being cited; any edition and volume statements; and the place, publisher, and date of publication. The inclusion of these data will help differentiate the volumes of the census published both by the government and by the private sector.

U.S. Census, 1790: Heads of Families. Washington: Government Printing Office, 1908.

US 8.22a Include a personal author if one is named.

U.S. Census, 1850: Statistical View of the United States . . . Compendium of the Seventh Census by J.D.B. DeBow. Washington: A.O.P. Nicholson, Public Printer, 1854.

US 8.22b In the early censuses statistics on manufactures, agriculture, housing, population, etc. were taken as part of the decennial census. Gradually various economic questions came to be covered in separate censuses. The first element in a citation to a modern census should be the type and year of the census. The name of the census should be taken directly from the publication. Include any volume numbers given before the title of the specific document.

U.S. Census of Manufactures, 1967: Vol. II, Industry Statistics: Pt. 1 Major Groups 20-24. Final Report. Washington: Government Printing Office, 1971.

US 8.22c If a census report number is given (usually on the upper left or right corner of the title/cover page), use it in the title statement.

> *U.S. Census of Population, 1970: Subject Reports: American*
> *Indians* (PC(2) — IF). Final Report. Washington:
> Government Printing Office, 1973.

US 8.22d The GPO has issued parts of the census on microfiche. When
you cite the census in a format other than paper, you should
include the medium as a part of the title statement (see US
2.9).

> *U.S. Census of Population and Housing, 1980: Block Statis-*
> *tics: Minnesota, Selected Areas.* (PHC 80-1-25; micro-
> fiche). Washington: Government Printing Office,
> 1982. (C3.229/5:PHC80-1-25).

US 8.22e It is also possible to have data from computer tapes. Since some
information is available only in a machine-readable format, be
sure to alert your reader to this.

> *U.S. Census of Population and Housing, 1980: Summary*
> *Tape File 2A and 2B* prepared by the Bureau of the
> Census (machine-readable data file). Washington:
> U.S. Bureau of the Census, 1981.

US 8.22f If applicable, you should specify when you are citing a preliminary, advance, or final report. This is basically an edition
statement and should be placed appropriately.

> *U.S. Census of Population and Housing, 1980: Final*
> *Population and Housing Unit Counts. Pennsylvania*
> (PHC 80-V-40). Advance Report. Washington:
> Government Printing Office, 1982.

US 8.22g Finally, much of the data of the census has been reproduced
and sold by groups other than the federal government. If you
use such a source, be sure to inform your reader in the imprint
data that you did not use the government version of a census or
census data. This is very important since frequently in these
publications the data has been manipulated or sorted to appear
in certain groupings which are *not* in the official census.

COMMERCIAL PUBLISHER
1980 U.S. Census Population and Housing Characteristics:

Place Data and Indices. San Diego: National Decision Systems, 1982.

STATE DATA CENTER PUBLICATION

Pennsylvania Municipalities: 1980 General Population and Housing Characteristics (PSDE 80-1-82). Middletown, Pa.: Pennsylvania State Data Center, 1982.

US 8.23   Statistical Abstract of the United States

One of the most enduring government documents and one of the most frequently used reference sources, the *Statistical Abstract* can be cited by giving title, edition, and imprint.

> *Statistical Abstract of the United States 1981.* 102nd ed. Washington: Government Printing Office, 1982.

US 8.23a If citing a specific table or data set from the book, give the name of the table followed by the pagination.

> "Normal Daily Maximum Temperature," p. 209. In *Statistical Abstract of the United States 1981.* 102nd ed. Washington: Government Printing Office, 1982.

US 8.24   Patents

To cite a patent granted by the U.S. government, you will probably have in hand either the patent itself or its abstract in the *Official Gazette.* In either case it is recommended that you give your reader the name of the invention, the inventor, the patent number, and the date granted. A citation to the abstract will also include a citation into the correct volume of the *Official Gazette.*

PATENT

> "Implement Wheel" by William Schumacher. U.S. Patent 4,376,554 (15 Mar. 1983).

OFFICIAL GAZETTE

> "Implement Wheel" by William Schumacher. U.S. Patent 4,376,554 (15 Mar. 1983), *Official Gazette of the United States Patent and Trademark Office* 1028:3(15 Mar. 1983) p. 517.

US 8.25 JPRS Reports

JPRS reports are primarily translations of print media. Usually several articles are grouped in each report, and the reports are grouped by geographic area. Information on the original source is found in the paragraph heading for each translation. For the microfiche edition you will have to look at the first frame of the translation to find this information. You should include personal author (if any), the title (shortened if necessary), the city and source of the original document, volume, date, and page numbers. When an entire book is translated, you should include all of the following (if given): author, translated title, original title, place, publisher, and date.

The second part of the citation describes the JPRS series. You should include the area name and report number (if they are given), the JPRS report number, and the date of the translation. This information can be found on the title page, the bibliographic data sheet, or on the microfiche header. In citing a GPO microfiche edition (the most widely used) give the microfiche number if there is more than one microfiche per report, and the page numbers on the microfiche. Finally, your citation should include a note containing either the SuDoc number or the Readex entry number.

PERIODICAL CITATION IN THE GPO EDITION

Konstandinou, T.S. "PASOK Positions on EEC
Membership Analyzed," Athens *Oikonomikos
Takhydromos* 46(12 Nov. 1981) pp. 23-26. Trans-
lation by the Joint Publications Research Service.
West Europe Report No. 1885, JPRS No. 79843; 12
Jan. 1982. (GPO microfiche; PrEx7.18:1885;
pp. 25-35).

BOOK CITATION IN READEX EDITION

*Subversion: Uruguayan Armed Forces Summary of Subversive
Movements in Latin America* (trans. of *La Subversion*).
Montevideo: Joint Chiefs of Staff, Uruguayan
Armed Forces, 1977. Translation by the Joint Pub-
lications Research Service. JPRS No. 69596-1; 12
Aug. 1977. (1978 Readex microprint 12212).

US 8.26   FBIS Reports

The FBIS reports are translations of written and spoken media messages picked up by 15 FBIS bureaus located throughout the world. These messages are usually translated from a foreign language into English, although occasionally the television/ radio transmissions are made initially in English. The reports themselves group these translations by geopolitical source and subject area. In citing an FBIS document take the information about the original document from the paragraph heading (Fig. 10).

US 8.26a For newspaper accounts the citation will be the same as JPRS citations: personal author, if any; title; an edition statement as to whether the translation is complete "text" or only "excerpts"; city and source; volume; date; and page number. This is then followed by a citation to the exact FBIS report which includes name, volume, issue, date, any locational notes, and pagination in the report.

> Simurov, A. and V. Yanovskiy. "We Have Come To Know Each Other Better; the Peace March–82 Has Ended" (text). Moscow *Pravda* (30 July 1982) p. 4. Translation by the Foreign Broadcast Information Service. *FBIS Daily Report — Soviet Union* Vol. III:150; 4 Aug. 1982 (GPO microfiche; PrEx7.10: FBIS-SOV-82-150; pp. AA7-11).

US 8.26b For television/radio broadcasts include personal author, title, edition statement (as above), the source and language in which the message was broadcast, and the date of broadcast in Greenwich Mean Time (GMT). All of this information is given in a line (or more) which precedes the translation. This is followed by a citation covering the exact FBIS report in which the translation can be found, including SuDoc number if available.

> MICROFICHE COPY
> Mnatsakonov, Edward. "The World Today" (text), Moscow Domestic Television Service in Russian, 1445 GMT 3 Aug. 1982. Translation by the Foreign Broadcast Information Service. *FBIS Daily Report — Soviet Union* Vol.III:150; 4 Aug. 1982. (GPO microfiche; PrEx7.10:FBIS-SOV-82-150; p. H14).

Page Number

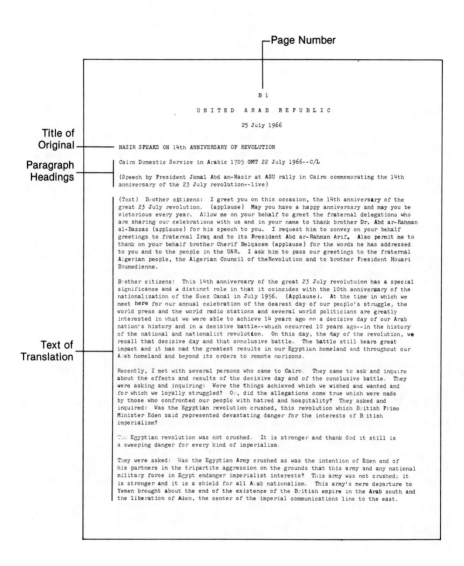

Title of Original

Paragraph Headings

Text of Translation

B 1

U N I T E D   A R A B   R E P U B L I C

25 July 1966

NASIR SPEAKS ON 14th ANNIVERSARY OF REVOLUTION

Cairo Domestic Service in Arabic 1705 GMT 22 July 1966--C/L

(Speech by President Jamal Abd an-Nasir at ASU rally in Cairo commemorating the 14th anniversary of the 23 July revolution--live)

(Text) Brother citizens: I greet you on this occasion, the 14th anniversary of the great 23 July revolution. (applause) May you have a happy anniversary and may you be victorious every year. Allow me on your behalf to greet the fraternal delegations who are sharing our celebrations with us and in your name to thank brother Dr. Abd ar-Rahman al-Bazzaz (applause) for his speech to you. I request him to convey on your behalf greetings to fraternal Iraq and to its President Abd ar-Rahman Arif. Also permit me to thank on your behalf brother Cherif Belqacem (applause) for the words he has addressed to you and to the people in the UAR. I ask him to pass our greetings to the fraternal Algerian people, the Algerian Council of theRevolution and to brother President Houari Boumedienne.

Brother citizens: This 14th anniversary of the great 23 July revolutuion has a special significance and a distinct role in that it coincides with the 10th anniversary of the nationalization of the Suez Canal in July 1956. (Applause). At the time in which we meet here for our annual celebration of the dearest day of our people's struggle, the world press and the world radio stations and several world politicians are greatly interested in what we were able to achieve 14 years ago on a decisive day of our Arab nation's history and in a decisive battle--which occurred 10 years ago--in the history of the national and nationalist revolution. On this day, the day of the revolution, we recall that decisive day and that conclusive battle. The battle still bears great impact and it has had the greatest results in our Egyptian homeland and throughout our Arab homeland and beyond its orders to remote norizons.

Recently, I met with several persons who came to Cairo. They came to ask and inquire about the effects and results of the decisive day and of the conclusive battle. They were asking and inquiring: Were the things achieved which we wished and wanted and for which we loyally struggled? Or, did the allegations come true which were made by those who confronted our people with hatred and hospitality? They asked and inquired: Was the Egyptian revolution crushed, this revolution which British Prime Minister Eden said represented devastating danger for the interests of British imperialism?

The Egyptian revolution was not crushed. It is stronger and thank God it still is a sweeping danger for every kind of imperialism.

They were asked: Was the Egyptian Army crushed as was the intention of Eden and of his partners in the tripartite aggression on the grounds that this army and any national military force in Egypt endanger imperialist interests? This army was not crushed; it is stronger and it is a shield for all Arab nationalism. This army's mere departure to Yemen brought about the end of the existence of the British empire in the Arab south and the liberation of Aden, the center of the imperial communications line to the east.

Fig. 10

FBIS Report Page

PAPER COPY

"Destroyer Sent to Beirut" (excerpts). Rome Domestic
Service in Italian, 2200 GMT 9 May 1983.
Translation by the Foreign Broadcast Information
Service. *FBIS Daily Report — Western Europe* Vol.
VII:91; 10 May 1983; p. A7.

US 8.27   Securities and Exchange Commission Reports

The Securities and Exchange Commission requires various
financial reports from companies selling stock on national ex-
changes. These reports vary in periodicity and content. The
best known is the annual 10-K report, but there are, among
others, 10-Q's, 8-K's, and 10-C's. These reports are all filed
with the SEC, and some are official company reports sent to
stockholders. All of them are filmed by private micropublishers. In citing one of these reports authorship should be
given to the company producing the report. The title, shortened if possible, should then follow. If you are citing the paper
version of the report, imprint data should include the year of
filing and the location of corporate headquarters.

> Singer Corporation. *Form 10-K Annual Report . . . FY
> Ended Dec. 31, 1982.* Stamford, Conn., 1983.

US 8.27a In citing a micropublisher's version of the report include the
micropublisher's filming date and name in a note following the
main part of the citation.

> Singer Corporation. *Form 10-K Annual Report . . . FY
> Ended Dec. 31, 1982.* Stamford, Conn., 1983. (1983
> Disclosure microfiche).

US 8.28   Clearinghouse Documents

The U.S. government has established more than 300 clearinghouses which gather and distribute information on various
topics. Clearinghouse documents may be unpublished reports,
contract reports, or reports previously published by non-
governmental and governmental organizations at all levels.
These documents are generally known as "technical reports,"
although their subject matter is frequently neither scientific nor
technical.

US 8.28a A citation to a contract report should include, as applicable: sponsoring agency; title; personal author, institutional affiliation, and location; report number; date; and a note including the abbreviated clearinghouse name and the report identification number (Fig. 5). If the medium is other than paper, it should be noted. (See also US 8.28e).

> U.S. Environmental Protection Agency. Office of Research and Development. *Evaluation of Solid Sorbents for Water Sampling* by J.C. Harris et al. of Arthur D. Little, Inc., Cambridge, Mass. (EPA-600/2-80-193). 1980. (NTIS PB 81-106585).

US 8.28b A citation to a government report should include, as applicable: issuing agency; title; personal authors, if any; imprint; series; and a note including the abbreviated clearinghouse name and the report identification number. If the medium is other than paper, it should be noted.

> U.S. Department of Health, Education and Welfare. Bureau of Occupational and Adult Education. *Counseling Implications of Re-Entry Women's Life Experiences* by Ruth Ekstrom et al. Washington: DHEW, 1980. (ERIC microfiche ED 209 600).

US 8.28c A citation to a non-governmental report should include, as applicable: personal author, title, imprint, series, and a note including the abbreviated clearinghouse name and the report identification number. If the medium is other than paper, it should be noted.

> Greeley, Andrew M. *The Rediscovery of Diversity.* Chicago: National Opinion Research Center, 1971. (ERIC microfiche ED 068 602).

US 8.28d A citation to an unpublished report should include, as applicable: personal author, title, date, and a note including the abbreviated clearinghouse name and report identification number. If the medium is other than paper, it should be noted.

> Basefsky, Stuart. *Bibliographic Citations and U.S. Government Publications.* 1979. (ERIC microfiche ED 223 251).

US 8.28e Some contract reports are distributed both by the GPO and by clearinghouses. If you have a document distributed by GPO (see US 4.2) which also has a clearinghouse "availability statement," you should alert your reader in a note to this dual distribution (Fig. 5).

> U.S. National Aeronautics and Space Administration. *Environmental Exposure Effects on Composite Materials for Commercial Aircraft* by Martin N. Gibbons and Daniel J. Hoffman of Advanced Structures, Boeing Commercial Airplane Co., Seattle, Wash. (NASA-CR-3502; microfiche). Washington: Government Printing Office, 1982. (NAS1.26:3502; also available NTIS NASA-CR-3502).

US 8.29   Commercial Publication Reprints as Federal Documents

The federal government infrequently distributes documents which have not been issued or written by an agency. In these cases an agency has partially sponsored the writing or development of the document, and the government reprints and distributes the commercial publication.

For such documents a citation to the item should include the personal author, title, edition, imprint, and series data, as applicable. Since there may be no straightforward indication that the government had any connection with the production of the document, a distribution and Superintendent of Documents classification note should be added alerting your reader that the item is also a government document.

> UNIVERSITY PRESS BOOK
>
> Shigo, Alex and Karl Roy. *Violin Woods: A New Look.* Durham, N.H.: University of New Hampshire, 1983. (Distributed by GPO; A13.2:V81).

> PRIVATE PUBLISHER REPRINT
>
> Quirk, James, Katsuaki Terasawa, and David Whipple. *Coal Models and Their Use in Government Planning.* New York: Praeger, 1982. (Distributed by GPO; NAS1.2:C63).

US 8.30   Microform Collections

Several commercial publishers distribute federal documents republished in microform and organized into collections. If you are using a document from such a collection, you must cite both the original document and the microform collection. The first part of the citation should contain a complete reference to the original paper document, taken from the title page frame of the microform. The information about the collection should be given in a note at the end. What information is given will depend on the organization of the collection. Use whatever information you used to locate the document in the microform collection.

US 8.30a Some collections are organized by year and by a filing control number assigned by the publisher.

> U.S. Department of Health, Education and Welfare. *The Measure of Poverty.* Washington: DHEW, 1976. (1976 ASI microfiche 4006-3).

US 8.30b Some collections follow the organization of the source from which they were filmed. The Greenwood Press microfiche collection was filmed from the Senate Library and uses the Senate volume number as an accession number. Since several documents may be found in one volume, you should also include the "tab" number for location on the microfiche.

> U.S. Senate. Committee on Labor and Public Welfare. *Mine Safety* Hearings, 18-19, 24-27, 31 May 1949. Washington: Government Printing Office, 1949. (81st Congress Greenwood Press microfiche S. Vol. 908-1).

US 8.31 Archives and Documents Originally Published in Microform Collections

Many government documents are never published in paper by the government. They would remain in archives or as unpublished papers were it not for micropublication. In citing such a document you must cite the microform collection as well as the document, since it is unlikely that your reader would ever find it except in the microform collection. This is in contrast to a republication on microform by a private publisher, such as CIS (see US 8.30). Give the issuing agency, title (shortened if necessary), place, and date of issuance for the original document. Then give the title and imprint of the collection and

whatever number (e.g., reel number, microfiche number) is
used to locate the document.

MICROFICHE COLLECTION
OF A COMMERCIAL PUBLISHER

U.S. Joint Chiefs of Staff. *Memorandum for the Deputy
Director for Intelligence . . . [on] Development of U.S.
Position on Zones of Occupation for Germany, 1943-44.*
Washington: 1952. In *Declassified Documents Reference
System, 1980.* Washington: Carrolton Press, 1980.
(Microfiche 42A).

MICROFILM COLLECTION
OF A COMMERCIAL PUBLISHER

U.S. Library of Congress. Congressional Research
Service. *Do We Really Need All Those Electric Plants?*
by Alvin Kaufman and Karen K. Nelson. 1982. In
*Major Studies and Issue Briefs of the Congressional
Research Service, 1982-83 Supp.* Frederick, Md:
University Publications of America, 1983. (Reel IV,
frame 278).

MICROFILM COLLECTION
BY A GOVERNMENT AGENCY

U.S. Census of Population, 1900. Schedule No. 1:
Allen Township, Northhampton County, Pennsylvania. In U.S. National Archives and Records Service. *Twelfth Census of the United States, 1900.*
Washington: NARS, 1973. (Reel 1446).

MICROFICHE COLLECTION
BY A GOVERNMENT AGENCY (see also US 8.28)

U.S. National Bureau of Standards. Center for Fire
Research. *Effect of Ventilation on the Rates of Heat,
Smoke and Carbon Monoxide Production in a Typical Jail
Cell Fire* by B.T. Lee. Washington, 1982. In U.S.
National Criminal Justice Reference Service.
Microfiche Collection (NCJ-84592).

US 8.32   Freedom of Information Act (FOIA)

For documents obtained under the Freedom of Information
Act (FOIA) you should try to identify the documents as
precisely as possible. This will depend on the nature of the

document and the amount of information given. Some elements which should be included are: personal author and
agency affiliation; title or subject; type of document, including
identifying numbers or other information; date; and number of
pages.

You should also name the agency from which you obtained the document, the nature of your request, the date of
your request, and the date of receipt. With this information
your reader could (theoretically) get the same documents.

LETTER

Hamilton, Donald R. U.S. Embassy, El Salvador.
[Subject: Roatan Island]. Letter to Stephen Dachi,
U.S. Information Agency; 2 Mar. 1983. 2 pp.
Obtained under the Freedom of Information Act
from U.S. Information Agency; requested as
"Materials on Radio Marti," May 1983; received
June 1983.

FORM (contract, requisition, etc.)

50 KW Antenna Design and Proposed Site Evaluation,
Antigua, W.I. Request for Supplies/Service; Order
No. A226842; 24 May 1982. 7 pp. Obtained under
the Freedom of Information Act from U.S. Infor-
mation Agency; requested as "Materials on Radio
Marti," May 1983; received June 1983.

MEMORANDUM

Fernandez, John. Conference by High-Ranking State
Department Officials on Radio Marti and the
Hawkins Bill (S. 602). Memorandum to Shay,
Rodriguez and Briss; 4 Mar. 1983. 3 pp. Obtained
under the Freedom of Information Act from U.S.
Information Agency; requested as "Materials on
Radio Marti," May 1983; received June 1983.

PAPER (no author given, no date)

Assessment of the Effect of Radio Free Cuba (RFC)
on the Second Session, Region II Medium Frequency Broadcasting Conference, Rio de Janeiro,
Nov. 1981. Working paper. n.d. 2 pp. Obtained
under the Freedom of Information Act from U.S.
Information Agency; requested as "Materials on

Radio Marti," May 1983; received June 1983.

PAPER (no author, omissions noted; date implied by text)

VOA Requirements in the Caribbean. Position Paper No. 5C [missing pages]. [1981?]. 6 pp. Obtained under the Freedom of Information Act from U.S. Information Agency; requested as "Materials on Radio Marti," May 1983; received June 1983.

TELEGRAM (include, if given, reference numbers, time, sender, and receiver)

International Telecommunications Union. Plenipotentiary Conference Nairobi . . . 952Z 5 Nov. 1982, 10322 (incoming telegram NAIROB28119). 3 pp. Obtained under the Freedom of Information Act from U.S. Department of State; requested as "Materials on Radio Marti," May 1983; received June 1983.

REPORT (include identifying number)

Castro on Radio Marti. 19 Aug. 1982 (Correspondent Rpt. #2-8806). 1 p. Obtained under the Freedom of Information Act from U.S. Information Agency; requested as "Materials on Radio Marti," May 1983; received June 1983.

US 8.33   Computerized Information

The federal government is moving toward more information being distributed and available only in machine-readable form. A citation to data from such files should include, as applicable: issuing agency; title, statements of responsibility for production, medium designation; edition statement, including date and statement of responsibility for revision; imprint information for place of production, name of producing organization, and date; and a note about location and name of the distributing agency. This information can be found both through the system's logon and its technical documentation.

U.S. Law Enforcement Assistance Administration. *Juvenile Detention and Correctional Facility Census of 1971* conducted by the U.S. Bureau of the Census (machine-readable data file). LEAA Rev. 1975 ed.;

revised by LEAA Data Archive and Research Sup-
port Center, University of Illinois, Urbana.
Washington: U.S. Bureau of the Census, 1971.
(Distributed by the LEAA Data Archive and
Research Support Center).

US 8.33a If you are citing an on-line file which changes continually, you
should include in the imprint segment the location and source
of the data file and, if given, the date to which the file is updated.

U.S. Patent and Trademark Office. *CASSIS* prepared
by the University Computing Company (machine-
readable data file). Washington: PTO, updated to
27 Feb. 1984.

Chapter 3

State, Local, and Regional Documents

State, local, and regional (SLR) documents are publications either written or funded by a governmental entity. State/territorial documents tend to be produced by all branches of the 50 state governments and U.S. territories. Local and regional documents generally are products of city councils, county governments, and economic or planning commissions. Usually SLR documents are not produced in great quantity and are not uniformly distributed; thus, locating them can be a major problem to the researcher. Consequently, any citation elements which facilitate location should be included.

SLR 1   ISSUING AGENCY

Just as for U.S. documents, use the issuing agency as the first element for an SLR document citation. The rationale for citing the agency is:

> 1) indexing in the major reference sources lists documents by issuing agencies (see Appendix B);

2) indicating that you are dealing with an SLR document may facilitate its location in a library, since these documents frequently are housed in separate library collections;

3) since many state and local agencies have no formal distribution program, crediting the agency may help your reader acquire the document from the appropriate agency;

4) until very recently SLR documents in a library's card catalog would have been entered under the agency's name.

SLR 1.1   Geographic/Political Designation

For any local, state, or territorial document the issuing agency statement should begin with the complete name of the geographic/political entity issuing the report. This can be abbreviated. Care should be taken that sufficient information is given so that geographic/political entities with similar names (e.g., Beaufort, N.C. and S.C.) are distinguishable.

LOCAL

Allentown, Pa. Urban Observatory. *An Analysis of Tire Service Delivery for Master Planning in Allentown, Pa.* 1977.

STATE

Utah. Highway Safety Division. *Utah Fatal Crash Analysis 1973-1979* by Stephen W. Glines. Salt Lake City, n.d.

TERRITORY

Virgin Islands. Bureau of Commerce. *Tourism for the 1980's.* Charlotte Amalie, 1977.

SLR 1.1a For regional documents the citation should begin with the name of the issuing agency. If the region is within one state, end this statement with a standard state abbreviation in parentheses.

Centre Regional Planning Commission (Pa.). *Prospects for Industrial Zoning.* State College, 1969. (Land Use Study 1).

SLR 1.1b If the state's name appears as part of the agency's name, omit the state abbreviation at the end.

> Southwestern Pennsylvania Planning Commission.
> *The Plan for the 80's.* Pittsburgh, 1979.

SLR 1.1c For regional organizations which cross state boundaries, the inclusion of a single geographic designation in this statement is impossible. Location of these organizations is found in the imprint (see SLR 4.1c).

> Rio Grande Compact Commission. *Report on Water
> Availability . . . to the Governors of Colorado, New
> Mexico, and Texas.* Santa Fe, N.M., 1981.

SLR 1.2   Single Issuing Agency

Since local and state governments ˚are constantly altering bureaucratic form and changing names, it is best to include in your citation all the hierarchical levels listed on the document, going from the largest to the smallest. This will enable your reader to find an agency in the standard reference sources (Appendix B) and may help locate a document if a name change has occurred.

> LOCAL
> New York, N.Y. Department of Transportation.
> Bureau of Highway Operations. *1982 Annual Condi-
> tion Report on Bridges and Tunnels.* 1983.

> STATE
> Georgia. Department of Human Resources. Division
> of Physical Health. *Georgia Vital and Health Statistics,
> 1978.* Atlanta, 1980.

SLR 1.2a For regional documents give the complete name of the agency, ending with an abbreviated state designation, as appropriate (see SLR 1.1a and b).

> Joint Planning Commission of Lehigh-Northampton
> Counties (Pa.). *Population Growth Trends, 1980.*
> Lehigh Valley, 1981.

SLR 1.2b Some SLR documents do not list an issuing agency on the cover or the title page. This frequently occurs on mimeographed documents or computerized printouts. If you are using such a document, it is best to give your reader an idea of the agency issuing the report, assuming you know it or can at least give an educated guess. In such a case, bracket the issuing agency's name. If you do not know the source, omit the agency statement and simply begin your citation with the title (see SLR 2.1).

> [Idaho. Department of Education.] *Fall Enrollment Report, 1982/83.* Boise, 1982.

SLR 1.3   Multiple Issuing Agencies

Sometimes more than one political body may be instrumental in the production of a document, as in a cooperative effort between a federal and a state/local agency (Fig. 11). Use the first agency listed as the issuing agency. If you feel acknowledgment of the cooperative effort is a significant fact, this can be included in a note (see SLR 6.2).

> Oklahoma. Department of Agriculture. Crop and Livestock Reporting Service. *Oklahoma Agricultural Statistics 1981.* Oklahoma City, 1982. (Produced as a cooperative effort with the U.S. Dept. of Agriculture).

SLR 1.4   Legislature as an Issuing Agency

All states have a legislative body in their governmental structure. The names of these entities differ (e.g., General Assembly, Legislature, Legislative Assembly), but the work done is the same (see SLR 8.5). Citing such documents first requires identification of the geographic area and the name of the entity.

> Virginia. General Assembly. Senate. *Virginia in Transition.* Richmond, 1975.

SLR 1.4a If the document is a product of a legislative chamber, committee, or group, this should be noted in the agency statement.

> California. Legislature. Assembly. Committee on Revenue and Taxation. *Alcohol Beverage Taxation: A Briefing Book* by David Doerr (874). Sacramento, 1981.

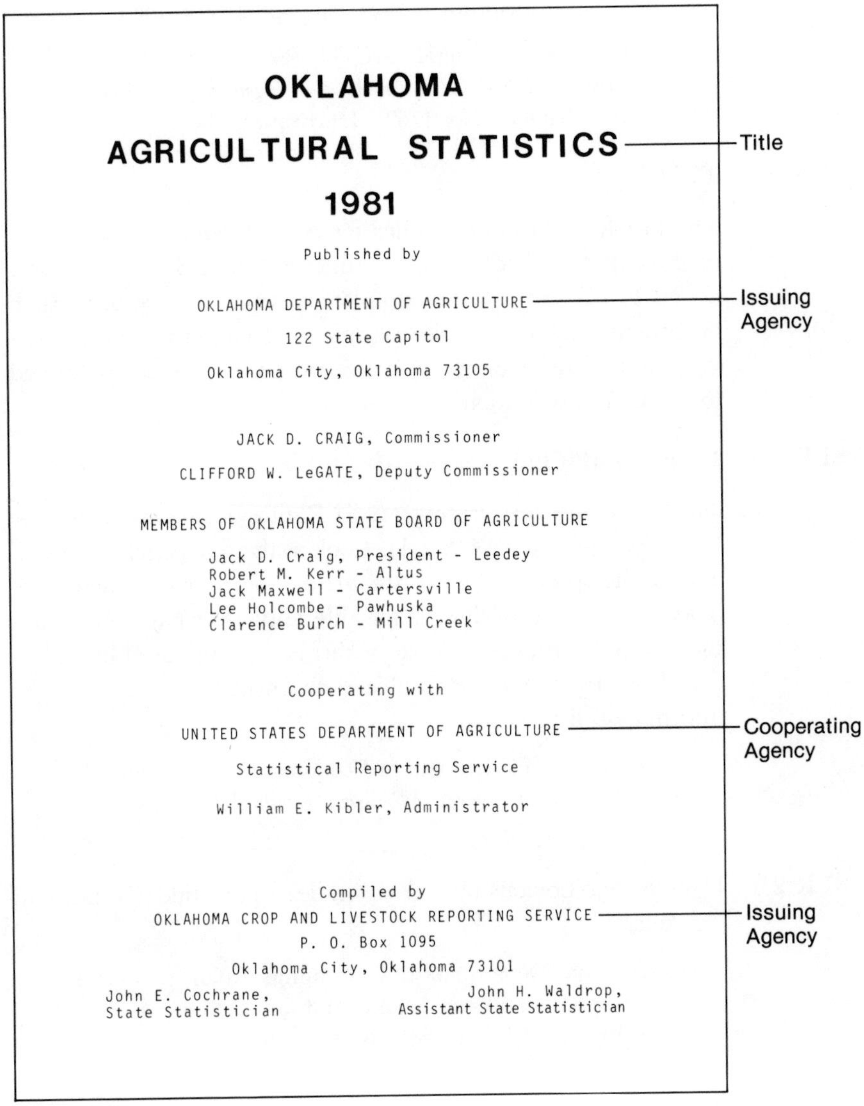

OKLAHOMA

AGRICULTURAL STATISTICS ——————Title

1981

Published by

OKLAHOMA DEPARTMENT OF AGRICULTURE ———————Issuing
Agency
122 State Capitol

Oklahoma City, Oklahoma 73105

JACK D. CRAIG, Commissioner

CLIFFORD W. LeGATE, Deputy Commissioner

MEMBERS OF OKLAHOMA STATE BOARD OF AGRICULTURE

Jack D. Craig, President - Leedey
Robert M. Kerr - Altus
Jack Maxwell - Cartersville
Lee Holcombe - Pawhuska
Clarence Burch - Mill Creek

Cooperating with

UNITED STATES DEPARTMENT OF AGRICULTURE ———————Cooperating
Agency
Statistical Reporting Service

William E. Kibler, Administrator

Compiled by
OKLAHOMA CROP AND LIVESTOCK REPORTING SERVICE ———————Issuing
Agency
P. O. Box 1095

Oklahoma City, Oklahoma 73101

John E. Cochrane,   John H. Waldrop,
State Statistician   Assistant State Statistician

Fig. 11
State Document: Title Page

SLR 1.4b If the document is a piece of legislation, the session, assembly, or meeting number should be included as part of the agency statement. Use this information as it appears on the document.

> Pennsylvania. General Assembly. Session of 1983.
> *House Bill No. 1456, An Act . . . Regulating Dog Racing* (Printer's No. 1769). Harrisburg, 1983.

SLR 2   TITLE

The problems in locating titles for SLR documents are similar to those outlined for U.S. documents (see US 2). However, added to this can be the complete absence of any title. Such documents are often mimeographed documents copied in a very limited number for in-house purposes and not published for general distribution.

SLR 2.1   Location of Title

The procedure for locating an SLR title is similar to that for U.S. documents (see US 2.1). Look at the title page, the cover, and/or the spine of the document, as appropriate. Choose the boldest statement of title. If the title and cover page differ, use the title page information, since this is the page used by indexers. If there is a bibliographic data sheet (Fig. 12), use the information listed there.

> Minnesota. Department of Economic Development. Research Division. *Minnesota Statistical Profile 1976.* St. Paul, 1976.

SLR 2.1a If there is no obvious title, devise a descriptive title and put it in brackets.

> Montana. Department of Community Affairs. Division of Research and Information Systems. [Profiles: Pondera County] (computer printout). 3rd ed. Helena, 1978.

SLR 2.1b If you are using a document on microfiche, be sure to use the title as it appears on the document; do not rely on the fiche header.

> Minnesota. Division of Fish and Wildlife. *1981 Big Game Hunting Regulations* (microfiche). St. Paul, 1981.

STANDARD TITLE PAGE FOR TECHNICAL REPORTS	1. Report No.	/////	3. Recipient Catalog No.
4. Title 1980 Technical Report			5. Report Date June, 1980
			6. Performing Org. Code
7. Author(s) Huntingdon County Planning Commission			8. Performing Org. Rpt No.
9. Performing Organization Name and Address Huntingdon County Planning Commission Court House Huntingdon, PA 16652			10. Project/Task/Work Unit No. * (See 15 Below)
			11. Contract/Grant No. CPA-PA-03 26 1135-36
12. Sponsoring Agency Name and Address Department of Housing and Urban Development 451 Seventh Street, S. W. Washington, D. C. 20410			13. Type of Report and Period Covered Final
			14. Sponsoring Agency Code

15. Supplementary Notes

  * (A) 0502.01; (B) 0503.02; (C) 1002.01; (D) 1102.01; (E) 0404.04

16. Abstracts
  - A. Housing Problem Definition (Housing Assistance Plan). This is a free-standing HAP for Huntingdon County.
  - B. Areawide Housing Opportunity Plan (AHOP). This County AHOP was included in Regional AHOP for Southern Alleghenies Region.
  - C. Service Level Analysis - Financial Analysis of Huntingdon County in the past and projections to 1986 as first step in the development of a capital improvements program.
  - D. Energy Legislation and Programs - Analysis of current energy legislation and listing of available funding programs for energy conservation.
  - E. Land Development Alternatives - Redesign of two subdivisions to show good development practices vs. bad development practices.

17. Key Words and Document Analysis. (a). Descriptors

17b. Identifiers/Open-Ended Terms

17c. COSATI Field/Group

18. Distribution Statement: Available to the Public From: Huntingdon County Planning Commission Court House Huntingdon, PA 16652	19. Security Class: (This Report) UNCLASSIFIED
	20. Security Class: (This Page) UNCLASSIFIED
	21. No. of Pages: 191
	22. Price: $5.00

FORM CFSTI-35 (4-70)   7/73

Title — 1980 Technical Report

Issuing Agency — Huntingdon County Planning Commission

Fig. 12

Bibliographic Data Sheet

SLR 2.2   Subtitles

Include a subtitle if it further defines or differentiates the subject of the document.

> Maryland. Department of State Planning. Office of
> Planning Data. *Maryland Population Data: County,
> MCD, and Municipal Trends Through 1980.* Baltimore,
> 1981. (Statistical Report Series 81-25).

SLR 2.3   Title Length

Titles which are excessively long can be shortened by the use of ellipses for omitted words (see US 2.3).

> Boston, Mass. *East Boston Capital Fund . . . Neighborhood
> Improvement Program.* 1979.

SLR 2.4   Language of Title

SLR documents may appear in a language other than English. If this applies to your document, give the title in the foreign language. A note can be added if the language is not obvious to the ordinary user (see SLR 6.2).

> Texas. Department of Health. *Disenteria Amibiana.*
> Austin, 1981.

SLR 2.5   Date in Title

If a date appears as part of the title, include it even if it is repeated in the publication data. The use of both dates will let your reader know that the document was published substantially after the time period covered.

> Alabama. Department of Archives and History.
> *Alabama Official and Statistical Register 1979.* Mont-
> gomery: Skinner Print Co., 1982.

SLR 2.6   Personal Authors

Include personal authors in the title statement, preceding the name with "by," "edited by," "prepared by," "compiled by," etc.

> Hawaii. Department of Land and Natural Resources.
> *The Kalia Burial Site: Rescue Archaeology in Waikiki* by

Earl Neller. Honolulu, 1980.

SLR 2.6a If the document was written by more than three people, simply give the first author listed on the document and cover the others by "et al." or "and others."

> Massachusetts. Division of Employment Security. *Occupational Profile of Selected Manufacturing Industries in Massachusetts 1980* prepared by Richard Sybrant et al. Boston, 1981. (Occupation/Industry Research Publication 14).

SLR 2.7 Contractors as Authors

Sometimes a government agency will contract with a private group to research a problem. Authorship should then be credited to this organization.

> Southwestern Pennsylvania Regional Planning Commission. *Directions in Housing Policies for Low and Moderate Income Families* ... prepared by the Institute for Urban Policy and Administration, University of Pittsburgh. Pittsburgh, 1972.

SLR 2.8 Agency Numbering Systems

Occasionally an SLR document will have a technical or agency report number printed on the cover, title page, or bibliographic information sheet. If so, include this number in the title statement in parentheses, following any personal authors (see US 2.8).

> Texas. Parks and Wildlife Department. Historic Sites and Restoration Branch. *Archeological Testing, Fanthorp Inn ... Grimes County, Texas* by R.E. Burnett (PWD 4000-294). Austin, 1981.

SLR 2.9 Medium

SLR documents appear in all possible forms, and your reader should be informed if the document you are citing is other than book form (see US 2.9). This is done by placing the information in parentheses after the title, personal authors, and agency number, as applicable.

MAP

Delaware River Basin Commission. *The Schuylkill River and Outdoor Recreation Area* (maps). West Trenton, N.J., 1983. (A cooperative publication with the Pennsylvania Department of Environmental Resources).

MICROFORM

Minnesota. Environmental Quality Board. *1979 Inventory of Power Plant Study Areas* (microfiche). St. Paul, 1979.

SLR 3   EDITION

An SLR document may be revised and reissued (see US 3). You should inform your reader which edition you are using in an edition statement.

SLR 3.1   Edition Statement

The edition statement should follow the title.

North Carolina. Department of Administration. Division of State Budget and Management. Research and Planning Services. *Profile: North Carolina Counties.* 5th ed. Raleigh, 1977.

SLR 3.1a If the edition is included either as part of the title or in an agency report number, you do not need to repeat the information in a separate edition statement.

Ozark Regional Commission. *The Consolidation of the Southeast Arkansas Solid Waste Authority: A Final Report.* Little Rock, Ark., 1981.

SLR 3.2   Limited Editions

SLR documents frequently are printed in a very limited quantity. If you are aware of this, inform your reader, since it may affect location of the document.

Illinois. Commerce Commission. Public Utilities Division. *Operating Statistics of the Telephone Companies in Illinois, Year Ended Dec. 1982.* Ltd. ed. Springfield, 1982.

SLR 3.3   Reprints

It is also possible that an item has been reprinted. This information should be included in your citation as an edition statement.

> Pennsylvania. Department of Education. Bureau of
> Curriculum and Instruction. *Han Hanh Duoc Gap*
> prepared by Bui Tri, Louisette Logan, and Fan-
> nette N. Gordon. Reprinted 1982. Harrisburg,
> 1980.

SLR 4   IMPRINT

Imprint data include place of publication, publisher, and date (see US 4).

SLR 4.1   Place of Publication

Publication place can most frequently be found in the mailing address on a document or in the agency's listing on the title page. For state and territorial documents assume the place of publication is the capital unless otherwise indicated. Since the state's name is in the agency statement, inclusion of the state in the imprint is superfluous.

> Rhode Island. Department of Economic Development.
> *Rhode Island Basic Economic Statistics 1979/80.* 7th ed.
> Providence, 1980.

SLR 4.1a If a state or territorial document was published in a city other than the capital, use the name of that city as the imprint location.

> Florida. Department of Agriculture and Consumer
> Services. *Florida Agriculture Statistics: Citrus Summary
> 1982.* Orlando, 1983.

SLR 4.1b For regional documents assume the place of publication is the city in which the regional organization's headquarters is located. This information is usually available on the title page. If the state location is listed in the agency statement, it can be omitted from the imprint.

> Triad Regional Planning Commission (N.C.).

> *Housing Restoration in the Central Piedmont Area.*
> Greensboro, 1976.

SLR 4.1c For multistate regional organizations, include both the name of the city and the state, since these data are not in the agency statement.

> Delaware River Water Authority. *Watershed Study for Southeast New Jersey* by Thomas Burnett. Philadelphia, Pa., 1983.

SLR 4.1d For local documents you can usually assume the item was printed in the issuing community and, since these data are in the agency statement, they can be omitted from the imprint. If the item was printed elsewhere, give that place in the imprint.

> PRINTED IN COMMUNITY
>
> Richmond, Va. Mayor's Office. *Budget for 1973.* 1972.
>
> PRINTED ELSEWHERE
>
> St. Paul, Minn. *Community Development Block Grant Funds: Program Years 1975-78.* Minneapolis, 1979.

SLR 4.2   Publisher

State and local governments, as well as regional organizations, usually do not have official publishers and therefore contract with various printers. Unless a specific private firm is mentioned, the printer can be omitted from a citation.

> NO PRINTER LISTED
>
> Colorado. Bureau of Investigation. *Crime in Colorado: Uniform Crime Report.* Denver, 1980.
>
> PRIVATE PRINTER
>
> Louisiana. Secretary of State. *Report of the Secretary of State . . . Jan. 1, 1979-Dec. 31, 1980.* Baton Rouge: Moran Industries, 1981.

SLR 4.3   Date of Publication

The date of publication on SLR documents can usually be found on the title page, in the preface, or in a letter of transmittal at the beginning of the document.

Maine. Department of Educational and Cultural
Services. State Library. *Libraries in Maine 1980-81.*
Augusta, 1981.

SLR 4.3a If no date can be found and the receipt date of the item was
stamped on the document, use that date, bracketed, with a
"by."

> Rhode Island. Department of Business Regulations.
> *72nd Annual Report of the Banking Division.* Pro-
> vidence, [by 1979].

SLR 4.3b If you cannot find a date, use n.d. (no date).

> Illinois. State Board of Elections. *A Candidate's Guide for
> 1982 Elections.* Springfield, n.d.

SLR 5   SERIES

SLR documents may be part of a series (see US 5). Such documents will have clear series statements on the title or cover
pages.

SLR 5.1   Series Name and Number

Include series name and number information in parentheses
following the imprint data.

> New Jersey. Department of Labor and Industry. *New
> Jersey Work Stoppages 1971.* Trenton, 1972. (Work
> Stoppage Series 2).

SLR 5.2   SLR Documents as Part of a Federal Series

If a document is prepared in cooperation with a federal agency,
the report may also have federal agency report numbers (see
US 2.8) or be part of a federal document series (see US 5). If
this is the case, this fact should be noted in either a title or series
statement.

> Florida. Department of Environmental Regulation.
> *Source, Use, and Disposition of Water in Florida, 1980*
> by Stanley Leach et al. Tallahassee, 1983. (U.S.
> Geological Survey. Water Resources Investigation
> 82-4090).

SLR 6   NOTES

For SLR documents the "notes" section of a citation may be optional or required, depending on the information to be included (see US 6).

SLR 6.1   Required Notes

Required notes are those which would denote looseleaf format, inclusion in a microform collection (see US 8.30), or mimeographed material.

> LOOSELEAF
>
> "Reducing, Suspending, or Cancelling Food Stamp Benefits" (Sect. 543, 9 Mar. 1981). In Pennsylvania Department of Public Welfare. Office of Family Assistance. *Public Assistance Eligibility Manual.* Harrisburg. (Looseleaf).
>
> MICROFORM COLLECTION NUMBERS
> (see also SLR 8.10)
>
> District of Columbia. Department of Employment Services. *Women in the Labor Force, Washington D. C. and Metropolitan Area 1979.* Washington, [by 1981]. (1981 SRI microfiche S1527-2).
>
> MIMEOGRAPHED MATERIAL
>
> Madison, Wis. Comptroller. *Financial Statements: Auditor's Report for the Year Ended Dec. 31, 1978.* 1979. (Mimeo).

SLR 6.2   Optional Notes

Optional notes are items covering cooperative publishing, language, map scale, or publication type (see US 6.2).

> COOPERATIVE AUTHORSHIP
>
> Oklahoma. Department of Agriculture. Crop and Livestock Reporting Service. *Oklahoma Agricultural Statistics 1981.* Oklahoma City, 1982. (Produced as a cooperative effort with the U.S. Dept. of Agriculture).
>
> LANGUAGE
>
> Texas. Department of Human Resources. *Chido en*

Hogar de Dia. Austin, n.d. (Spanish).

MAP SCALE

Alaska. Division of Geological and Geophysical
Surveys. *Geologic and Materials Maps of the Anchorage
C-7SE Quadrangle* by C.L. Daniels (map). Juneau,
1981. (1:2400).

PUBLICATION TYPE

Pennsylvania. Department of Community Affairs.
Financing Parks and Recreation Facilities in Pennsylvania.
2nd ed. Harrisburg, 1980. (Pamphlet).

SLR 7   CITING PARTS: ARTICLES, CHAPTERS, AND LOOSELEAFS

If you have a periodical article or a chapter in a document
issued by a state, territorial, local, or regional government, you
have different citation elements to consider.

SLR 7.1   Periodicals

In a periodical citation you must include the personal author,
the article's title, the title of the periodical, volume, issue
number, date, pagination, and source of the periodical. It is
very important that a source note be included to alert your
reader to the fact that the item is a government document (see
US 7.1).

> Jones, Marie. "Postwar Baby Boom Shifts 80's Labor
> Supply," *Prairie Employer Review* 3:11(Nov. 81) p. 1.
> (Publication of the North Dakota Job Service).

SLR 7.1a If there is more than one author, use the rules outlined in
US 7.1b.

SLR 7.1b If there is no personal author, begin the citation with the title of
the article.

> "Governor Cites State ERA at Congressional Hear-
> ings ...," *Womenews* 7:1(Sept.-Oct. 83) p. 1.
> (Publication of the Pennsylvania Commission for
> Women).

SLR 7.2 Non-periodicals

If you have a part of a document to cite, the process is slightly different (see US 7.2). Include the author/title of the part being cited, as applicable; pagination for the part; and citation to the item as a whole.

> "The Halfmoon Township Comprehensive Plan,"
> pp. 145-156. In Centre Regional Planning Commission (Pa.). *The Planning Document.* State College, 1976.

SLR 7.3 Looseleafs

A citation to an SLR looseleaf publication requires the same elements as any looseleaf document (see US 7.3).

> "Chapter 5-1300: Fire Exits" (Supp. 4, 1975). In Philadelphia, Pa. *Philadelphia Code.* (Looseleaf).

SLR 8 SPECIAL CASES

Certain SLR documents are so frequently cited, are so well known, or present such unique problems that they are best covered in a separate section.

SLR 8.1 State Blue Books

State "blue books" are government documents which cover various types of information. Usually they provide background data about a state and its government. To cite "blue books" give the issuing agency; title; personal author, if any; and any relevant imprint data.

> Oklahoma. State Election Board. *Directory of Oklahoma 1981.* Oklahoma City, 1981.

SLR 8.1a Some blue books are not written or published by the state but by a private individual or group. Credit should then be given to the private group or publisher.

> Arizona. Department of State. *Bill Turnbow's 1977-78 Arizona Political Almanac* edited by Mrs. Bill Turnbow. Phoenix, 1977.

SLR 8.2   State Laws

Each state issues volumes containing its laws. A citation to a state law should include the law's name and number, if given; date of passage; the volume number and name of the legal set in which the law can be found; and pagination.

> "An Act Providing for Post Conviction Hearings . . ."
> (Act 294, 30 Nov. 1967), *Laws of Pennsylvania* 67,
> p. 639.

SLR 8.2a To cite a law before it appears in final book form, give the name, jurisdiction, and number of the law and its date of passage.

> "An Act Concerning Game and Other Wild Birds and
> Animals" (Pennsylvania Act No. 1983-28, 20 July
> 1983).

SLR 8.3   State Regulations

States promulgate regulations to uphold the laws. The citation form will depend on the item in hand. If you have the complete regulations of the state in a bound or looseleaf format, give the name of the regulation; date of promulgation, if known; the name of the book in hand; and any section/title numbers. If the item is in looseleaf format, this should be noted.

> "Discharges to Underground Waters," Nov. 1981,
> *Pennsylvania Code,* Title 25, Sect. 97.33. (Looseleaf).

SLR 8.3a If you have a document which lists proposed or enacted regulations and which updates the bound or looseleaf edition, give the name of the regulation, action sought, the name of the volume, volume/issue numbers, date, and pagination.

> "Surface and Underground Coal Mining, proposed
> rule to amend 25 Pa. Code Ch. 86," *Pennsylvania
> Bulletin* 13:39(24 Sept. 1983) pp. 2896-2898.

SLR 8.4   Local Ordinances

Local ordinances should be cited in a manner similar to state regulations. Again, the exact elements of the citation will depend on the item in hand. Include those elements which would help actually locate the ordinance within the larger document. Usually you should have the title and internal report numbers, date, and the title of the volume in which the information can be found.

> "Speed Limits Established" (Chap. 16, Pt. 2, Sect. 12, 12 Aug. 1975), *Code of Ordinances of the Township of Patton* (Pa.). State College: Penns Valley Publishers. (Looseleaf).

SLR 8.5   Legislative Documents

All state legislative document citations should begin with the name of the state and its legislative body. Further hierarchical breakdowns to chamber, committee, and subcommittee should be included in the author statement.

> Florida. Legislature. House of Representatives. Committee on Community Affairs. *Oversight Report: Local Government Comprehensive Planning Act.* Tallahassee, 1982.

SLR 8.5a In most states bills introduced in each legislative session are numbered sequentially; consequently, the same numbers are used every year. Therefore, it is necessary to alert your reader in the author statement to the legislative session, if possible. Use the session numbers or years as they appear on the document. If this information is not on the document, the imprint date will have to suffice.

> California. Legislature. Assembly. 1981/82 Regular Session. *AB 3797 Flame Retardant Roofs.* Sacramento, 1982.

SLR 8.5b Some states assign printing or report numbers to legislative documentation. If these numbers are helpful in locating or differentiating among similar items, such as amendments to a bill, they should be included in the title statement as agency numbers. If they are not useful as location devices, they may be omitted. If you are unsure about their value, it is best to include them.

> PRINTER'S NUMBER
> Pennsylvania. General Assembly. Session of 1983.

> *Senate Bill 1099, An Act Relating to the Public School System* . . . (Printer's No. 1406). Harrisburg, 1983.

REPORT NUMBER

> California. Legislature. Assembly. Committee on Revenue and Taxation. *Implementation of Proposition 13* by Bob Leland (No. 748). Sacramento, 1979.

SLR 8.5c In many states legislative documents, particularly hearings, are not printed or distributed by the government. The documents are available only from the stenographic firm which transcribed the session. Should this be the case facing you, include in the imprint the name and location of the stenographic firm so your reader will have a potential source for the document.

> Florida. Legislature. House of Representatives. Select Committee on Reapportionment. *Subcommittee on Congressional Redistricting Meeting, 8 Mar. 1982.* Tallahassee: Southern Reporting Services, 1982.

SLR 8.6 Statistical Abstracts

Most states produce an annual statistical abstract. Although these documents are usually written by a state agency, sometimes universities or private organizations become involved in the production of the abstract. A citation to such reference sources should give the issuing agency or group, title, edition, and imprint data.

> Delaware. Office of Management, Budget, and Planning. *Dimensions on Delaware: A Statistical Abstract for 1979.* Dover, 1980.

SLR 8.6a A citation to specific data should list the table name, volume, and pagination.

> "Milk Cows on Farms . . . 1970-82," p. 298. In University of North Dakota. Bureau of Business and Economic Research. *North Dakota Statistical Abstract 1983.* 2nd ed. Grand Forks, 1983.

SLR 8.7 State Data Center Publications

State data centers are cooperative enterprises between state governments and the U.S. Bureau of the Census. The goal of these organizations is to distribute census data more efficiently and economically to end users. One method of attaining this goal is to issue special census analyses of computer data for states. The reports should be cited as state reports, including issuing agency, title, report numbers, and imprint data.

> Pennsylvania. State Data Center. *Pennsylvania Municipalities: 1980 General Population and Housing Characteristics* (PSDC80-1-82). Middletown, 1982.

> Texas. State Data Center. *Final Population and Housing Counts for Texas Cities, Counties, SMSA's.* Austin, 1981.

SLR 8.8   University Publications

In most states there is at least one state university whose operation is supported partially by state funding. Theoretically, any documents produced at these institutions are also state documents. However, in most libraries such reports would not be in a separate document collection, but would rather be cataloged with the main collection. Therefore, the best way to cite these documents is to give credit to the personal author(s) first, followed by title, edition, imprint data, series, and notes.

> Cato, James C. and Frank J. Lawlor. *Small Boat Longlining for Swordfish on Florida's East Coast.* Gainesville, Fla.: University of Florida, 1981. (Florida Sea Grant College. Marine Advisory Bulletin 2604).

SLR 8.8a Universities occasionally publish documents for state agencies as "university press books." This information should be included in the imprint statement.

> North Carolina. Department of Cultural Resources. Division of Archives and History. *The Quest for Progress: The Way We Lived in North Carolina, 1870-1920* by Sydney Nathans. Chapel Hill: University of North Carolina, 1983.

SLR 8.9   Agricultural Experiment and Extension Publications

The U.S. government has established throughout the country cooperative intergovernmental organizations which deal with agriculture and home economics. These agencies are known generally as "ag extension services" and "agricultural experiment stations.'' Any citation to documents produced by these agencies should list the standard citation elements of issuing agency, title, edition, imprint, series, and notes.

> Connecticut. Agricultural Experiment Station. *Quality of Chip Dips* by Lester Hankin, Donald Shields, and J. Gordon Hanna. New Haven, 1981. (Bulletin 794).

SLR 8.9a Many universities serve as agricultural extension services and experiment stations. Citations to publications issued directly from these organizations should cite the university as the issuing agency, with personal authors added in the title statement.

> Montana State University. Cooperative Extension Service. *Farm and Home Security* by Roy Linn. Bozeman, 1982. (Circular 1017).

SLR 8.10 Microform Collections

Some SLR documents have been reprinted by commercial micropublishers. If you are using a document republished in microform, cite the document as if it were in paper form and include the micropublisher information in a note.

> Vermont. Secretary of State. *Primary and General Elections Vermont 1980 Including Presidential Preference Primary* prepared by the Vermont Elections Project. Burlington, Vt.: University of Vermont Agricultural Experiment Station, 1981. (1981 SRI microfiche S8115-1).

> Philadelphia, Pa. City Planning Commission. *Philadelphia Center City Walking Tour.* 1976. (Urban Documents Microfiche Collection PPA-0227).

SLR 8.11 Clearinghouse Documents

Just as in U.S. technical report documentation, there are cases in which SLR reports are distributed by a national clearinghouse, such as NTIS (see US 8.28). If you know that your document is available through such an entity, include this information in a note.

> Pennsylvania. Governor's Justice Commission. *Comprehensive Plan for the Improvement of Criminal Justice in Pennsylvania.* Harrisburg, 1978. (NTIS microfiche PB 284 551).

SLR 8.12 State Freedom of Information Material

Most states have a statute similar to the federal Freedom of Information Act through which citizens can request unpublished state documents. The citation elements for such documents are similar to those for FOIA material: personal author, state, and agency affiliation, if applicable; title or subject; document type; any identifying numbers; date; pagination; agency from which the material was requested; nature of the request; date of request; and date of receipt (see US 8.32).

LaVine, William. Pennsylvania. Department of Environmental Resources. Kepone Levels in Spring Creek. Report and Data Gathered from Last Fish Kill, May 1981. 7 pp. Obtained under the Pa. Open Records Act; requested as "Spring Creek Kepone Levels," June 1981; received Dec. 1981.

Chapter 4

International Documents

"International documents" are the publications and documentation of international intergovernmental organizations. *Not* included in this category are publications of non-governmental international organizations or those of national governments.

Unlike U.S. federal documents, there is no "universal system" of organizing international documents. Consequently, you should provide as many access points as you reasonably can.

The majority of citations will include the issuing agency, a title, a document number (if given), place of publication, publisher, and date. For some agencies, like the UN, a document number is a good access point to indexes and collections; for others whose only access is a sales catalog, a title and a date of publication are important access points; for still others there are no catalogs and no indexes and, thus, finding them will be a matter of a particular library's way of handling them.

I 1   **ISSUING AGENCY**

The issuing agency, and not the personal author, should be the first element in a citation to an international document because:

1) many documents do not have personal authors;
2) even when they do, many indexes and catalogs do not use the personal author in their indexing;
3) to be consistent with citation forms for other documents, the issuing agency should be used;
4) giving the issuing agency as author immediately signals your readers that they are looking for an international document (i.e. that they may not find it through the usual library channels).

Citing the personal authors of parts of documents is an exception to this rule (see I 7).

This looks unorthodox for some citations, but it serves a purpose. In the usual citation form for books (author, title, imprint) the organization's role may be completely ignored. One case in point is the report of Unesco's "MacBride Commission." It is often cited as:

> *Many Voices, One World.* New York: Unipub, 1980.

This is fine for libraries which have it cataloged. However, it does not allow for any access in those libraries which have chosen to keep it in a separate international documents collection. Therefore, a better citation — one that would allow for a variety of locations — is:

> U.N. Educational, Scientific, and Cultural Organization. International Commission for the Study of Communication Problems. *Many Voices, One World.* New York: Unipub, 1980.

I 1.1   Single Issuing Agency

A citation begins with the name, in full, of the organization.

> Food and Agriculture Organization of the United Nations. *A Zambian Handbook of Pasture and Fodder Crops.* Rome, 1979.

I 1.1a

If more than one level in the hierarchy is given, all should be used, from the largest to the smallest unit.

> U.N. Economic and Social Council. Committee on

Natural Resources. *Mineral Resources: Trends and
Salient Issues with Particular Reference to Rare Metals,
Report of the Secretary General* (E/C/1983/8). 6 Apr.
1983. (Mimeo).

I 1.1b   When the agency is not listed on the document, but you know
its name from another source, include it in brackets. It may
save your reader a lot of work searching for the location of an
obscure office.

U.N. Educational, Scientific, and Cultural Organiza-
tion. [Secretariat. Sector for Programme Support].
Organization of Unesco Secretariat Since 1946
(PRS.79/WS/47). Paris, 1979.

I 1.2   Multiple Issuing Agencies

When confronted with a document issued cooperatively by
more than one agency, use the agency which seems to
dominate (e.g., the organization which published it), and list
the other agency in a note (see I 6.1d). You cannot be sure
under which agency a library will list it or whether either
agency will list it in its catalog.

Food and Agriculture Organization of the United
Nations. *Fish Feed Technology* (ADCP/REP/80/11).
Rome, 1980. (Aquaculture Development and Coor-
dination Programme Series). (Joint Project with
United Nations Development Programme).

I 1.3   Abbreviations and Acronyms

Except for the United Nations (UN) you should not assume
that every reader knows the full title of such common acronyms
as UNESCO or WHO. Spell out the name in the issuing
agency statement. If the name appears in the title, take it exactly as given.

Southeast Asian Ministers of Education Organization.
Resource Book on SEAMEO (SEAMES/SPIP-1/1981).
Bangkok, 1981.

I 1.4   Language of the Issuing Agency

There are three general rules for deciding which name to use for multilingual organizations:

1) Do not make your own translations. If you must use a language other than the one used in the document in hand, take the name from the *Yearbook of International Organizations* (Appendix B).
2) Use the name in the language you are using for the rest of your bibliography, if such a name exists.
3) Be consistent; use the name in the same language throughout, even if the texts of the documents are in different languages. Using a single form of the issuing agency's name assures that all publications for the agency will be together in an alphabetically arranged bibliography and will be less confusing to your reader.

IN AN ENGLISH-LANGUAGE BIBLIOGRAPHY

Organization of American States. General Secretariat. *Report on the Situation of Human Rights in the Republic of Guatemala* (OEA/Ser.L/V/11.61; Doc.47, rev.1). Washington, 1983.

THE SAME DOCUMENT IN A SPANISH-LANGUAGE BIBLIOGRAPHY

Organizacion de los Estados Americanos. Secretaria General. *Report on the Situation of Human Rights in the Republic of Guatemala* (OEA/Ser.L/V/11.61; Doc.47, rev.1). Washington, 1983.

I 1.5   Parliamentary Body as Issuing Agency

Many international organizations have bodies which meet regularly. These may be called meetings, assemblies, conferences, and so forth. In citing documents which come from these parliamentary bodies you should give the parent organization, the name of the group and any numerical designator the organization uses, and the date of the meeting as it is given on the document. This may be a year, month, and day or days. As a general rule, it is best to follow the practice of the organization.

International Labour Organization. International Labour Conference, 69th Session, 1983. *Report VII: Social Aspects of Industrialisation.* Geneva, 1983.

I 1.5a   If the document comes from a smaller group within the body, include this group in the citation.

> U.N. General Assembly, 37th Session. First Committee. *Verbatim Record of the 59th Meeting*, 9 Dec. 1982 (A/C.1/37/PV.59). Official Record. 18 Jan. 1983.

I 1.5b   If a city is named as the meeting place, include it. For organizations which meet in different places from year to year, this may be important information in locating the document.

> U.N. Educational, Scientific, and Cultural Organization. General Conference, 21st Session, Belgrade, 1980. *Records of the General Conference: Vol. 3 Proceedings*. Paris, 1982.

I 1.5c   If the group and session number are not explicitly mentioned, but you can deduce them from other data (such as a report number), include them in brackets.

> International Atomic Energy Agency [General Conference, 27th Regular Session]. *The Agency's Budget for 1984* (GC(XXVII)/686). [Vienna] Austria, 1983.

I 1.5d   Look at the arrangement of the organization's meetings. If, in order to distinguish one publication from another, you need to include more information about the session, do so. In the following example, it is necessary to give the part number because there are three different volumes for texts adopted in the 34th session.

> Council of Europe. Parliamentary Assembly, 34th Session, 3rd Pt. "Opinion #112 (1983) on the texts adopted at the 17th Session of the Conference of Local & Regional Authorities of Europe," *Texts Adopted by the Assembly*. Strasbourg, 1983.

I 2   **TITLE**

Titles of international documents range from the very obvious to the very obscure and even to the non-existent. The following rules are meant to give some guidance when you have conflicting information or when it is not apparent what the title is.

I 2.1   Title Page

If the document has different titles on the title page, the front cover, and the spine, use the title as it is given on the title page.

> Council of Europe. European Committee on Crime Problems. *Aspects of the International Validity of Criminal Judgments.* Strasbourg, 1968.

I 2.1a   If the document is on microfiche, take the title from the appropriate frame and *not* from the microfiche header. The form of titles on microfiche headers is dictated by the space available and does not always agree with the title page.

> Organisation for Economic Cooperation and Development. *Controls and Impediments Affecting Inward Direct Investments in OECD Member Countries* (21-82-06-1; microfiche). Paris, 1982.

I 2.1b   If the document has "Cataloging in Publication" (CIP) or a bibliographic sheet (Fig. 13), use the title as given there.

> European Communities. Commission. *The Old World and the New Technologies: Challenges to Europe in a Hostile World* by Michel Godet and Olivier Ruyssen (CB-30-80-116-EN-C). Rev. ed. Luxembourg: Office for Official Publications, 1981. (European Perspectives Series).

I 2.2   Subtitles

Use a subtitle if it will help distinguish common titles or if it will help explain the title's relevance to your research.

> World Health Organization. *On Being In Charge: A Guideline for Middle-level Management in Primary Health Care* by Rosemary McMahon, Elizabeth Barton, and Maurice Piot. Geneva, 1980.

I 2.3   Title Length

If a title is very long, you need not give the whole title. *Do not,* however, leave out words in the beginning of the title or any important descriptive words. Omitted parts should be indicated with ellipses (. . .). *Explanatory Report on the Protocol Amending the Convention of 6 May 1963 on the Reduction of Cases of Multiple*

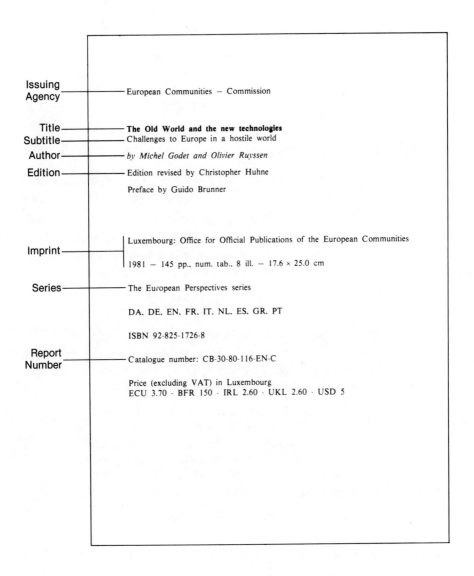

Issuing Agency ——————— European Communities — Commission

Title ———————— **The Old World and the new technologies**
Subtitle ———————— Challenges to Europe in a hostile world
Author ———————— *by Michel Godet and Olivier Ruyssen*
Edition ———————— Edition revised by Christopher Huhne

Preface by Guido Brunner

Imprint ———————— Luxembourg: Office for Official Publications of the European Communities

1981 — 145 pp., num. tab., 8 ill. — 17.6 × 25.0 cm

Series ———————— The European Perspectives series

DA, DE, EN, FR, IT, NL, ES, GR, PT

ISBN 92-825-1726-8

Report Number ———————— Catalogue number: CB-30-80-116-EN-C

Price (excluding VAT) in Luxembourg
ECU 3.70 - BFR 150 - IRL 2.60 - UKL 2.60 - USD 5

Fig. 13
CIP Bibliographic Slip

Nationality and Military Obligations in the Case of Multiple Nationality and Explanatory Report on the Additional Protocol to the Convention of 6 May 1963 on the Reduction of Cases of Multiple Nationality and Military Obligations in Cases of Multiple Nationality may safely be reduced to:

> Council of Europe. *Explanatory Report on the Protocol Amending the Convention of 6 May 1963 on the Reduction of Cases of Multiple Nationality and Military Obligations . . . and . . . on the Additional Protocol . . . .* Strasbourg, 1978.

I 2.4   Language of Title

Use the title in the language as given. Do not translate titles even if you give the author and publisher data in your own language (see I 1.4).

> European Communities. Commission. *Kodifizierungssystem fur forstliches Vermehrungsgut. B. Artikelhauptkatalogue* (CB-NA-78-037-DE-C). Luxembourg: Office for Official Publications, 1978. (Reihe mitteilungen uber Landwirtschaft 57).

I 2.4a   If the publication is multilingual, you do not need to give the title in all the languages listed on the document. Use the title in the language of your bibliography or, if no title is given in that language, use the title in the language you read.

> European Communities. Commission. Statistical Office. *Tax Statistics, 1970-1976* (CA-22-77-613-6A-C). Luxembourg: Office for Official Publications, 1977. (Macroeconomic statistics — purple series).

I 2.5   Date in Title

Include dates used in titles and underline them as part of the title. At times the date may be repeated as the publishing date, but frequently the two dates are not the same (see example in I 2.4a).

I 2.5a   For conferences, workshops, and symposia give the place and date after the title but do not underline them.

> Council of Europe. *Proceedings of the European Population*

Conference, 1982 Strasbourg, 21-24 Sept. 1982. Strasbourg, 1983.

I 2.6   Personal Authors

Although personal authors are not usually mentioned in the "documentation" (i.e. working papers) of international organizations, many "publications" (i.e. works created for public sale) do have personal authors. In some libraries sale publications may be treated like other books and may be included in the library's catalog under title and personal author, while in others they may be kept in a separate collection by organization. Because there is no single standard and no way of predicting how such a document will be found, you must be sure both the agency and the personal author's name are given. Place the agency's name first, to conform with other document citations, then the title followed by the personal author.

> Council of Europe. Council for Cultural Cooperation.
> *Innovation in Secondary Education in Europe* by R.A.
> Wake, V. Marbeau, and A.D.C. Peterson. Strasbourg, 1979.

I 2.6a   When there are more than three personal authors, give the name of the first and include the others under "et al." or "and others" (see US 2.6a).

> World Fertility Survey. *The Fiji Fertility Survey: A Critical Commentary on Administration and Methodology — Appendices* by M.A. Sahib et al. London, 1975. (Occasional Paper No. 16).

I 2.7   Titles of UN Mimeographed Documents

Titles of UN mimeographed documents are often extremely long, confusing in form, and not very informative (Fig. 14). Because of this and because the exact title is not very useful in locating UN "mimeos," it is permissible to shorten it with ellipses (. . .) or to create a title (in brackets) giving the subject of the document when no meaningful title exists. This is more informative for readers and will not affect their ability to locate the document.

More important is the series/symbol number. It should

Publication
Date

Series/
Symbol
Number

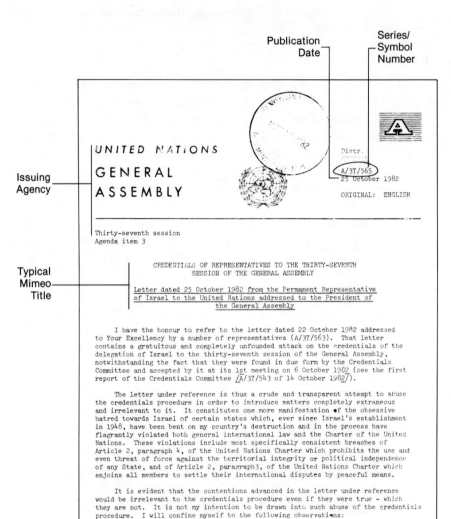

Issuing
Agency

Typical
Mimeo
Title

Fig. 14
UN Mimeo

be included after the title. Other information — place and publisher — may be omitted from citations to the paper copy since it is not given on the document. (For citation to the Readex microprint edition see I 2.9.) Publication day, month, and year come next. Finally, you should indicate that it is a mimeographed document.

> U.N. General Assembly, 37th Session. *Letter . . . 25 October 1982 from the Permanent Representative of Israel . . . [on the Attack on Credentials of the Israeli Delegation]* (A/37/565). 25 Oct. 1982. (Mimeo).

I 2.8   **Organizational Numbering Systems**

A few international organizations have devised numbering schemes which they print on some of their documents. Because this number may be useful in some indexes and in some libraries and because each number is unique to a given document, it should be included in parentheses after the title.

Table 3

ORGANIZATIONAL NUMBERING SYSTEMS

Organization	Example	Place
United Nations	A/37/565 (see I 2.7)	On mimeo documents in the upper right corner of the first page (see Fig. 14). On *Official Records,* either upper right corner or under title on cover page. On Secretariat (ST/) and other documents may be on back of title page.
European Communities	CA-22-77-613-6A-C (see I 2.4a)	Any or all of the following: back cover, back of title page, bibliographic slip, or cataloging in publication (see I 2.2) on last page. Often pre-

ceded by Kat./Cat./
(Fig. 13).

Organisation for Economic Cooperation and Development (OECD)	21-82-06-1 (see I 2.1a)	Lower left corner of back cover, small type in parentheses, or last frame of microfiche.
Organization of American States (OAS)	OEA/SER.L/V/ 11.61 (see I 1.4)	Usually on title page; sometimes also on spine.
Food and Agriculture Organization (FAO)	ADCP/REP/80/11 (see I 1.2)	On title or cover page.
International Atomic Energy Agency (IAEA)		
Documents:	INFCIRC/306 (see I 4.1a)	On upper right corner of first page.
Publications:	STI/PUB/498 (see I 7.2)	On back of title page for whole publications.
	IAEA-SM-232/65 (see I 7.2)	On first page of article for individual articles.
United Nations Educational, Scientific, and Cultural Organization (UNESCO)	PRS.79/WS/47 (see I. 1.1b)	On lower left or upper right corner of first page; used on documents only, not on Unesco Press publications.

I 2.9   Medium

Like U.S. government documents, international documents come in a variety of media (see US 2.9). You should indicate after the title when the medium is anything other than the traditional book format, unless it is indicated by some other part of the citation.

MICROFICHE

Organisation for Economic Cooperation and Development. *Household Waste: Separate Collection and Recycling* (97-82-09-1; microfiche). Paris, 1983.

MICROFICHE REPUBLISHED IN COLLECTION

International Telecommunications Satellite Organization. *IntelSat: Annual Report, 1982.* Washington, 1982. (1983 IIS microfiche 2090-S1).

MICROFICHE ORIGINAL IN COLLECTION

International Labour Office. World Employment Programme. *Education and Employment: A Synthesis* by Jan Verslius (WEP 2-18/WP 19). Geneva, 1979. (WEP Research Working Papers in Microfiche Form 1978).

MICROPRINT (Readex edition)

U.N. General Assembly, 36th Session. *Preliminary List of . . . the Provisional Agenda of the 36th Regular Session . . .* (A/36/50). 15 Feb. 1981. (1982 Readex microprint).

MIXED MEDIA

U.N. Educational, Scientific, and Cultural Organization. MAB, Programme on Man and the Biosphere. *Man and the Humid Tropics* by L. Hamilton (slide-tape). Paris: Unesco Press, 1979. (MAB Audio-visual Series 1).

REALIA (things)

U.N. [Secretariat]. Office of Public Information. *Flag and Map Kit* (realia). New York, 1976. (Sales No. E/F 76.I.3).

MAP

U.N. *A Student Map of the United Nations* (map no. 2753, rev. 4). New York, 1978. (Sales No. E.78.I.11).

FILM

U.N. Centre for Human Settlements (HABITAT). *Action in Rural Living Areas* (film). Nairobi, 1976. (16mm., 15 min., col.).

I 3   EDITION

The edition should be cited if there is a likelihood that more than one edition has been issued or will be issued at some time.

I 3.1   Edition Statement

The edition as given on the document should be cited after the title.

> World Meteorological Organization. Secretariat. *Guidelines for the Education and Training of Personnel in Meteorology and Operational Hydrology* (WMO-No.258). 2nd ed. Geneva, 1977.

I 3.1a   If it is evident from the title or from a report number, the edition need not be cited after the title data.

> EDITION AS PART OF TITLE
>
> Organisation for Economic Cooperation and Development. International Institute for Refrigeration. *Draft Code of Practice for Frozen Fish* (53-69-01-3). Paris, 1969.

> EDITION AS PART OF REPORT NUMBER
>
> European Communities. Commission. *Commission's Proposals to the Council [on] . . . Generalized Tariff Preferences . . . 1982 to 1985 . . .* (COM(81)422 final). Brussels, 1981.

I 3.1b   UN Official Records also constitute a final edition of many UN mimeographed documents. For instructions on their citations see I 8.2.

I 4   IMPRINT

Imprint consists of place of publication, publisher, and date of publication.

I 4.1   Place of Publication

Give the name of the place in full (i.e. city and country) unless it is so well-known that it cannot be mistaken.

> U.N. Institute for Namibia. *Toward a Language Policy*

for Namibia: English as the Official Language, Perspectives and Strategies. Lusaka, Zambia, 1981. (Namibia Study Series No. 4).

I 4.1a If the place is not given, write n.p. (no place). You cannot assume that a document comes from the headquarters city since international organizations have too many branches in too many locations.

> International Atomic Energy Agency. *The Text of the Agreement Between Colombia and the Agency for . . . Safeguards . . . [re] the Treaty for the Prohibition of Nuclear Weapons in Latin America* (INFCIRC/306). n.p., 1983.

I 4.2 **Publisher**

If the document names a publishing office of the organization, give that.

> European Communities. Commission. *Women and the European Community: Community Action, Comparative National Situations* (CB-24-78-281-EN-C). Luxembourg: Office for Official Publications, 1980.

I 4.2a When no special publishing agency within the organization is named (as opposed to the Office for Official Publications of the European Communities, for example), assume that the publisher is the organization. Its name need not be repeated.

> Council of Europe. European Public Health Committee. *Family Planning.* Strasbourg, 1977.

I 4.2b If the work comes from Unesco in Paris and looks like a commercial book (i.e., it has a fancy cover, is typeset rather than photoreproduced from a typescript, and has a title page and a Unesco copyright), it is probably from Unesco Press. To distinguish it from other Unesco publications which are *not* from Unesco Press, you should use the Press as the publisher.

> U.N. Educational, Scientific, and Cultural Organization. *The Book Today in Africa* by S.I.A. Kotai. Paris: Unesco Press, 1981.

I 4.2c Some international documents are published for the organization by commercial or university presses.

> World Bank. *Yugoslavia: Development with Decentralization*
> by Vinod Dubey et al. Baltimore: Johns Hopkins
> University Press, 1975.

I 4.3   Date of Publication

The date of publication will usually be found on the title page
or on the back of the title page. You need use only the year in
most cases.

> U.N. Educational, Scientific, and Cultural Organiza-
> tion. Asian Programme of Educational Innovation
> for Development. *Biology Education in Asia: Report of
> a Regional Workshop* Quezon City, Philippines, 18-23
> Aug. 1980. Bangkok: Unesco Regional Office for
> Education in Asia and the Pacific, 1980.

I 4.3a   If no date is given, but the document has a library date stamp,
write [by year]. This will at least allow your reader to narrow
the search.

> Inter-American Development Bank. *Fifteen Years of
> Activities, 1960-74.* Washington, [by 1976].

I 4.3b   If you cannot find any date, write "n.d."

> U.N. Relief and Works Agency for Palestine Refugees
> in the Near East. *Opportunity.* n.p., n.d.

I 4.3c   You should omit place and publisher for UN mimeos.
However, you must give a complete date. The publication date
can be found under the series/symbol number (Fig. 14). Ignore
other dates for the imprint; they may be used, as appropriate,
in other parts of the citation.

> U.N. Economic and Social Council. Committee on
> Natural Resources. *Mineral Resources: Trends and
> Salient Issues, with Particular Reference to Rare Metals:
> Report of the Secretary-General* (E/C.7/1983/8). 6 Apr.
> 1983. (Mimeo).

I 5   SERIES

A series is a group of publications under one group title with distinct titles for individual works. They may or may not be numbered. It is a good idea to include series information in a citation because:

1) it is often a shortcut in locating the document;
2) if a bibliographic record (index, card catalog, etc.) does not distinguish individual titles in a series, the series name may be the *only* way of locating it.

I 5.1   Series Name and Number

Name and number, if applicable, should come in parentheses after the imprint data.

> U.N. [Secretariat]. Department of Social Affairs. Population Branch. *Age and Sex Patterns of Mortality: Life Tables for Under-developed Countries* (ST/SOA/ Ser.A/22). New York, 1955. (Population Studies No. 22).

I 5.1a   If a document belongs to more than one series, cite all the applicable series.

> Food and Agriculture Organization of the United Nations. *Pesticide Residues in Food: Report of the 1976 Joint Meeting of the FAO Panel of Experts on Pesticide Residues and the Environment and the WHO Expert Group on Pesticide Residues,* Rome, 22-30 Nov. 1976. Rome, 1977. (FAO Food and Nutrition Series No. 9; FAO Plant Production and Protection Series No. 8; World Health Organization Technical Report Series No. 612). (Published jointly with WHO).

I 6   NOTES

Some useful information does not fit logically into any of the previous sections. This kind of information should be placed in parentheses at the end of the citation. Depending on the data, notes may be required or optional.

I 6.1   Required Notes

Required notes are those which may help your reader locate the document.

I 6.1a   Microform collection accession numbers should be given because such collections are arranged by the accession number.

IIS MICROFICHE

International Telecommunications Satellite Organization. *IntelSat: Annual Report, 1982.* Washington, 1982. (1983 IIS microfiche 2090-51).

FAO DOCUMENTATION MICROFICHE
COLLECTION

Food and Agriculture Organization of the United Nations. Forestry Department. *Basic Technology in Forest Operations (Equipment)* by R. Silversides and G. Segerstroem (microfiche). Rome, 1982. (FAO Forestry Paper No. 36). (FAO Acc. No. 8331507).

I 6.1b   Include the UN sales number in a note when there is no series/ symbol number. The sales number may be found on the back cover or on the back of the title page.

U.N. Department of Public Information. *Basic Facts About the United Nations.* New York, 1980. (UN Sales No. E.80.I.5).

I 6.1c   Mimeographed documents should be noted because this will affect your reader's ability to locate them. "Mimeos" are often reproduced only in small quantities and distributed to a few people. It is a good idea to warn your reader that a document may not be in wide circulation. Another category of mimeos is comprised of UN documents which are neither sales publications nor official records. These are not at all difficult to find, but telling your readers they are mimeos will send them directly to an established category of UN documentation.

UN MIMEOS

U.N. Third Conference on the Law of the Sea. *Delegations to the Third . . . Conference . . . : Sixth Session,* New York, 23 May to 15 July 1977 (A/Conf.62/INF.7). 21 June 1977. (Mimeo).

OTHER MIMEOS

Food and Agriculture Organization of the United Nations. Food Preservation Study Group. *Study of*

> *Crop Losses in Storage, State of Zacatecas, Mexico 1965-1975* by Hugo Perkins et al. n.p., 1976. (Mimeo).

I 6.1d If a document is produced jointly by more than one organization, use the most prominent (see I 1.2) as issuing agency/author and include any others in a note.

> U.N. General Assembly, 38th Session. [Iranian aggression against Iraq] *Letter dated 6 June 1983 from the Permanent Representative of Iraq . . . to the Secretary General* (A/38/267; S/15824). 14 June 1983. (Mimeo; issued jointly with the U.N. Security Council, 38th Year).

I 6.2 **Optional Notes**

Optional data are those which may give your reader a clue about the nature or characteristics of a document or information which is only marginally useful in locating the document.

I 6.2a Many international publications destined for sale are given an International Standard Book Number (ISBN), usually on the back cover or the back of the title page. This number may be helpful in identifying the publication, but it will not give the average user much help in locating it. Therefore, its use is optional.

> U.N. Educational, Scientific, and Cultural Organization. *Learning and Working.* Paris: Unesco Press, 1979. (ISBN 92-23-101684-9).

I 6.2b Map scale may tell your reader if a map has enough detail.

> European Communities. Commission. *The European Community: Member States, Regions and Administrative Units* (map). Luxembourg: Office for Official Publications, 1981. (1:8000000).

I 6.2c Film size, running time, and color or black and white may tell your readers if a film can be used for their purposes.

> U.N. Centre for Human Settlements (HABITAT). *Housing in Africa* (film). Nairobi, 1976. (16mm., 15 min., col.).

I 7   CITING PARTS: ARTICLES, CHAPTERS, SPEECHES, PAPERS, LOOSELEAFS

In citing a part of a publication, you must use both the title of the part and the title of the whole. You would cite a part in a bibliography when you are referring to a journal article; to an encyclopedia article; to legal and legislative material in collections; or to any kind of material published in a collection, such as a yearbook or an almanac.

I 7.1   Periodical Citations

A periodical citation should include the name of the author, the title of the article, the title of the journal, the volume and issue numbers (if it has these), the date of issue, and the page numbers. It should also include, for UN periodicals which have them, the series/symbol number. Finally, unless the periodical is very well-known or the organizational source appears in another element of the citation, you should add a note about the issuing organization.

> PERIODICAL ARTICLE; PERSONAL AUTHOR; LITTLE-KNOWN JOURNAL
>
> Wood, J. Duncan. "The Second Special Session on Disarmament: Some Hopes and Expectations — An NGO View," *Disarmament* 5(May 1982) pp. 31-40. (Publication of the United Nations).

> PERIODICAL ARTICLE; ORGANIZATIONAL AUTHOR; SERIES/SYMBOL NUMBER
>
> U.N. Secretariat. Department of International Economic and Social Affairs. Population Division. "The Demographic Situation in Developed Countries," *Population Bulletin of the United Nations* 12(1979) pp. 41-62. (ST/ESA/SER.N/12).

> PERIODICAL ARTICLE; NO AUTHOR
>
> "The Community and Events in the Middle East," *Bulletin of the European Communities* 13:9(1980) pp. 7-8.

I 7.2   Non-periodical Citations

> PAPER IN PROCEEDINGS
>
> Moghissi, A.A. "Biological Half Life of Tritium

in Humans" (IAEA-SM-232/65), pp. 501-507. In
International Atomic Energy Agency. *Behaviour of
Tritium in the Environment: Proceedings of a Symposium,
San Francisco, 16-20 Oct. 1978* (STI/PUB/498).
Vienna, 1979. (Proceedings Series).

ENCYCLOPEDIA ARTICLE

"Abattoirs," pp. 1-3. In *Encyclopedia of Occupational
Health and Safety*. 3rd ed. Geneva: International
Labour Organisation, 1983.

ARTICLE OR SECTION OF A YEARBOOK

"Third United Nations Conference on the Law of the
Sea," pp. 120-131. In *Yearbook of the United Nations,
1979*. New York: UN, 1982.

SINGLE CHAPTER WITH PERSONAL AUTHOR

Carrion, Alejandro. "Ecuador," pp. 15-24. In
Organization of Petroleum Exporting Countries.
Public Information Department. *Not Oil Alone: A
Cultural History of OPEC Member Countries*. Vienna,
1981.

SPEECH IN PARLIAMENTARY PROCEEDINGS

Mitterand, Pres. Francois. Speech, 30 Sept. 1982,
pp. 291-299. In Council of Europe. Parliamentary
Assembly, 34th Ordinary Session. *Official Report of
Debates*. Strasbourg, 1982.

I 7.3   Looseleaf Publications

A few international documents come in looseleaf format so that
they can be easily updated. The date of updating pages, which
will usually be found in the top or bottom margin, should be
included in the citation. Data about the location of the part
within the looseleaf will depend on the organization of the
looseleaf; it may be expressed in pages, sections, paragraph
labels, etc.

"Agreement in the form of an exchange of letters
between the European Economic Community and
Turkey on imports into the Community of un-
treated olive oil ... 1 Nov. 1977 to 31 Oct. 1978"
(Sect. Gen. 1, p. 1; 30 June 1979). In European

Communities. Council. *Collected Acts: Association Between the European Economic Community and Turkey,*
Vol. 2. n.p.: Secretariat of the Council of the European Communities. (Looseleaf).

I 8   SPECIAL CASES

The citations in this section cover:

1) titles which are so well-known that they do not require
   as much citation data as other documents;
2) international documents which present unique problems and therefore require special data elements;
3) international documents which are frequently cited
   and for which this section provides a quick reference.

I 8.1   League of Nations

League of Nations documents fall into two classes: "official
publications" and documents which were issued by League
agencies, such as the Information Section, but which are not
considered official.

I 8.1a   Official documents carry the official publication number,
usually in the upper right-hand corner of the title page. It
designates to whom the document was distributed, in what
sequence, in what year, and in what subject category. Put it
after the title in parentheses. This number is used for classification in many League documents collections. You may also find
series numbers which you should include in their appropriate
place.

> League of Nations. *How To Make the League of Nations
> Known and To Develop the Spirit of International Coopera-
> tion* (C.515.M.174. 1927.XIIA). Geneva, 1927.
> (Publications of the League of Nations XIIA Intel-
> lectual Cooperation C.I.C.I. 190).

I 8.1b   For some conference documents the official publication
number may not be indicated on the document. In that case,
give as much information as you can find on the document —
dates of the meeting, conference number, sales number (if
any).

League of Nations. Conference for the Reduction and
Limitation of Armaments. *Verbatim Record (Revised)
of the 18th Plenary Meeting* . . . 23 July 1932 . . .
(Conf.D/PV.18). n.p., 1932. (Sales No.
1932.IX.60).

I 8.1c   If you are citing a League document from a microform collection, cite the document and then the collection, giving the location of the document in the collection.

League of Nations. *Protection of Minorities in Poland: Peti-
tion and Annexes,* 23 June 1931 (C.306.1932.IB and
C.306(1).1932.IB). Geneva, 1932. In *League of
Nations Documents, 1919-1946.* New Haven, Conn.:
Research Publications, 1975. (Reel 1B-18).

I 8.1d   When citing an unofficial publication, be as specific as you can
about the issuing agency. You will not find League numbers
(see I 8.1a) on unofficial publications.

League of Nations. Secretariat. *The Aims, Methods
and Activity of the League of Nations.* Rev. ed. Geneva,
1938.

I 8.2   **UN Official Records**

Three types of UN official records are issued: supplements,
meeting records, and annexes. Supplements contain reports of
various bodies to the session. Meeting records are verbatim or
summary records. Annexes may contain other material, such
as a list of agenda items. In some sessions there may also be
documents not assigned to any of these categories, such as a list
of delegations or resolutions and decisions of the Security
Council.

I 8.2a   For a supplement, you should cite: the organ and session
number, the title and supplement number, the series/symbol
number, official record, and the imprint data.

U.N. General Assembly, 37th Session. *Report of the
Human Rights Committee* Supp. No. 40 (A/37/40).
Official Record. New York, 1982.

I 8.2b   For a meeting record you should cite: the organ and session number, the subsidiary group (if applicable), the title and meeting date, the series/symbol number, and official record. The imprint data will be limited to the date of publication, usually found under the series/symbol number.

> U.N. General Assembly, 38th Session. Special Political
> Committee. *Summary Record of the 48th Meeting,*
> 9 Dec. 1983 (A/SPC/38/SR.48). Official Record.
> 19 Dec. 1983.

I 8.2c   Annexes usually come in groups. For these you should cite the organ and session number, the agenda item number and title, annexes, official record, and imprint data taken from the title page of the annex (not from the first page of the agenda item number).

> U.N. Economic and Social Council, 55th Session.
> "Agenda Item 5: The Problem of Mass Poverty
> and Unemployment in Developing Countries,"
> *Annexes.* Official Record. New York, 1974.

I 8.2d   For documents which do not fall into any of these categories you should give: the organ and session number, the title and series/symbol (if any), official record, and the imprint data.

> U.N. Security Council, 32nd Year. *Resolutions and*
> *Decisions of the Security Council 1977* (S/INF/33).
> Official Record. New York, 1978.

I 8.2e   If any of the above are in microform, be sure to note that fact after the title data for the UN edition and in a note for any other.

> UN MICROFICHE
>
> U.N. Security Council, 32nd Year. *Resolutions and*
> *Decisions of the Security Council 1977* (S/INF/33;
> microfiche). Official Record. New York, 1978.
>
> READEX MICROPRINT EDITION
>
> U.N. General Assembly, 37th Session. *Report of the*
> *Human Rights Committee* Supp. No. 40 (A/37/40).
> Official Record. New York, 1982. (Readex micro-
> print).

I 8.3 **UN Resolutions**

The citation for a particular resolution will depend on where you found it, but it should contain enough information to allow your reader to find it in other places. You should include the name and session number (if given) of the organ and the subsidiary body and meeting number (if applicable). The next element is the number, title, and date of the resolution. Not all resolutions have titles. If this is the case with the document you are citing, make up a descriptive title and place it in brackets. From this point the citation will depend on whether you are citing a separate mimeographed document, the official record, or a commercially published collection.

I 8.3a For a separate "mimeo," add the series/symbol number after the title and "mimeo" at the end.

> U.N. Security Council, 2288th Meeting. "Resolution 487 (1981) [On the Israeli Air Attack on Iraqi Nuclear Installations]" (S/Res/487). 19 June 1981. (Mimeo).

I 8.3b For a resolution in the official records give the title, series/symbol number, official record, imprint for the official record, and the page numbers.

> U.N. Security Council, 22nd Year. "Resolution 242 [The Situation in the Middle East]" 22 Nov. 1967, pp. 8-9. In *Resolutions and Decisions of the Security Council 1967* (S/INF/22/Rev.2). Official Record. New York, 1968.

I 8.3c For a resolution from a commercially published collection add the bibliographic data for the collection.

> U.N. General Assembly, 24th Session. "Resolution 2603 Question of Chemical and Bacteriological (Biological) Weapons," 16 Dec. 1969, pp. 226-227. In *United Nations Resolutions, Series I General Assembly,* Vol. XII. Dobbs Ferry, N.Y.: Oceana, 1975.

I 8.3d For resolutions on microform add the medium statement after the series/symbol number for UN microfiche or in a note for the Readex microprint.

UN MICROFICHE

U.N. Security Council, 2288th Meeting. "Resolution 487 (1981) [On the Israeli Air Attack on Iraqi Nuclear Installations]" (S/Res/487; microfiche). 19 June 1981. (Mimeo).

READEX MICROPRINT EDITION

U.N. Economic and Social Council, 62nd Session. "Resolution 2086 (LXII) Infringements of Trade Union Rights in Southern Africa" (E/Res/2086 (LXII)). 23 May 1977. (Readex microprint).

I 8.4   **UN Conferences**

UN conference documents will be cited much like other UN documents, as official records or as "mimeos." The conference, its place, and its date are cited as the issuing agency. If "Official Record" appears as part of the title, it need not be repeated in the edition statement.

MIMEO

U.N. Conference on Desertification, Nairobi, Kenya, 29 Aug.–9 Sept. 1977. *Case Study of Desertification: Mona Reclamation Experimental Project Pakistan* (A/CONF.74/13). n.d. (Mimeo).

OFFICIAL RECORD

U.N. Conference to Consider Amendments to the Single Convention on Narcotic Drugs, 1961, Geneva, 6-24 Mar. 1972. *Official Records, Vol. I: Preparatory and Organizational Documents; Main Conference Documents; Final Act and Protocol . . .; Annexes* (E/CONF.63/10). New York, 1974.

I 8.5   **Annual Compendia of the UN and UN Affiliated Organizations**

The following titles are so well-known that you need cite only the title, date, and imprint data: *Yearbook of the United Nations; Statistical Yearbook* (UN); *Statistical Yearbook* (UNESCO); *Demographic Yearbook.*

Statistical Yearbook, 1981. New York: United Nations, 1983.

I 8.6   **UN Treaty Series**

Give the parties, the name or type of agreement, the place and date of signing, the UN registry number, the name of the series, volume, date, and page numbers.

> Brazil and Uruguay. Cultural Agreement, signed at Montevideo, 28 Dec. 1956 (No. 11951). *United Nations Treaty Series* 836(1972) pp. 3-23.

I 8.7   **International Court Reports**

International court reports should all follow the same general form: name of case; type (decision, order, judgment) and date of case; the name and volume of the reporter; and pagination. Some typical examples are given below.

I 8.7a   **INTERNATIONAL COURT OF JUSTICE REPORTS**

The reports of the International Court of Justice at the Hague are published in two forms — as slip opinions and in bound compilations. The citation is identical for both. The information can be found on the back of the title page.

> Continental Shelf (Libyan Arab Jamahiriya/Malta), Order of 26 Apr. 1983, *International Court of Justice Reports 1983,* pp. 3-4.

I 8.7b   **EUROPEAN COMMUNITIES COURT OF JUSTICE REPORTS**

The year on the cover should be used as the volume number; the issue number need not be used since the pagination is continuous throughout the year.

> Pierre Favre v Commission of the European Communities, Order of 7 Feb. 1983, *European Communities Court of Justice Reports 1983,* pp. 199-201.

I 8.7c   **REPORTS OF THE EUROPEAN COMMISSION AND COURT OF HUMAN RIGHTS**

Citations to cases reported in the *Yearbook of the European Convention on Human Rights* should include, after the type of agreement, whose decision (the Commission's or the Court's) is being reported.

> X and Y v Ireland (Decision of the Commission, 10 Oct. 1980), *Yearbook of the European Convention on Human Rights 1981,* pp. 132-204.

I 8.7d   Citations to cases reported in *Publications of the European Court of Human Rights* present special problems because this publication is not organized like other court reporters. It has two series — judgments and pleadings. The same case may appear in either series a number of times over a number of years. For these reasons you should cite, in addition to the basic elements given under I 8.7, the series and the imprint data. You can omit pages because each volume is devoted to a single case.

> Case of Young, James, and Webster (Judgment of 18 Oct. 1982), *Publications of the European Court of Human Rights: Series A: Judgments and Decisions* Vol. 55. Strasbourg: Council of Europe, Registry of the Court, 1983.

I 8.7e   For Series B there will be a range of dates instead of a date of decision. Include this after the series name.

> Sunday Times Case, *Publications of the European Court of Human Rights: Series B: Pleadings, Oral Arguments and Documents (1977-1980)* Vol. 28. Strasbourg: Council of Europe, Registry of the Court, 1982.

I 8.8   OAS Official Documents (Records)

To cite official records of the Organization of American States you should give, as applicable: the full name of the issuing body (including the number, date, and place for meeting records); the title and date of the document; its OAS classification number; official record; and the place and year of publication (if known).

> Organization of American States. Inter-American Nuclear Energy Commission, 10th Meeting, 11-15 July 1977, Lima, Peru. *Final Report* (OEA/Ser.C/ VIII.10). Official Record. Washington, 1977.

I 8.8a   If you are citing an official document in the microfiche collection, you must add the year, the name of the collection, and the microfiche filing number. You can omit "Official Record" as an edition since it will be given as the title of the collection.

> Organization of American States. Ministers of Foreign
> Affairs, 17th Meeting of Consultation, 21 Sept.
> 1978, Washington, D.C. *Note from the Ambassador*
> *... of Nicaragua Requesting Distribution of the Note ...*
> *Concerning Document OAS/Ser.L/V/II.45 ... "Report*
> *on ... Human Rights in Nicaragua"* 15 Feb. 1979
> (OEA/Ser.F/II.17; Doc.27/19). Washington, n.d.
> (1979 OAS Official Records microfiche 79-00002).

I 8.9   **Official Journal of the European Communities**

A citation to the *Official Journal* should contain some kind of title for the action. If it is taken exactly as given, it should be surrounded by quotation marks. If it is a composed title, it should be in brackets. You can also shorten a long title with ellipses. Any reasonable form is acceptable; your choice should be governed by the needs of your paper and by the nature of the title being cited. If you take it as given, do not translate or change punctuation or capitalization. Before 1972 there is no official English version; therefore, you will be citing an edition in French or some other official language.

I 8.9a   Before 1967 the rest of the citation will be much like a periodical citation with name, volume/issue number, date, and pages.

> "Resolution portant avis du Parlement Europeen sur
> la proposition de directive concernant les problemes
> sanitaires dans les echanges de produits a base de
> viandes," *Journal Officiel des Communautes Europeennes*
> 7:109(9 July 1964) p. 1710.

I 8.9b   From 1967 on the *Official Journal* is split into four parts: the C (Communications) series; the L (Legislative) series; the Supplement; and the Annex (debates of the European Parliament). For the first two you should give the L or C issue number after the title; this will signal your reader to look in Part C or Part L.

> "Commission Regulation (EEC) No. 71/80 of 15 Jan.
> 1980 altering the import levies on products proc-
> essed from rice or cereal," *Official Journal of the Euro-*
> *pean Communities* L 11(16 Jan. 1980) pp. 12-13.

I 8.9c   In citing the microfiche edition, you should also give the microfiche number.

> Written Question No. 190/76 ... 21 May 1976 [on Birth Grants], *Official Journal of the European Communities* C 7(9 Jan. 1978) pp. 1-2. (1978 O.J. microfiche no. 3).

I 8.9d   In citing the debates of the European Parliament before 1967 you will find no indication that they are part of the *Official Journal.* Therefore, you should cite the title given on the document.

> "Expose de M. le President de la Haute Autorite," *Assemblee Parlementaire Europeenne: Debats* 3(mai-juin 1958) pp. 7-16.

I 8.9e   However, if you are using the microfiche edition for those same years, you can cite the *Official Journal* in the microfiche note.

> "Allocution de M. le President de l'Assemblee," *Assemblee Parlementaire Europeenne: Debats* 1(mars 1958) pp. 30-32. (1958-59 *Journal Officiel: Debats* microfiche 1).

I 8.9f   From 1967 on, the debates have been issued as an annex to the *Official Journal.* "Debates" should be cited as a subtitle.

> "Organ transplants," *Official Journal of the European Communities, Annex: Debates of the European Parliament* 297(11-15 Apr. 1983) pp. 268-269.

I 8.9g   Citations to the supplement follow the same form as I 8.9f, except that an S-number is given in place of a volume number.

> "Public Works Contracts," *Official Journal of the European Communities,* Supp. S 105(4 June 1983) pp. 5-6.

I 8.10   European Parliament Working Documents

Cite the title of the individual document (shortened, if necessary) and cite *Working Documents* as a series with the document number. Give the full publication date; no other imprint information is provided.

> European Communities. European Parliament. *Report*

Drawn Up ... on Persons Missing in Argentina. 24 Oct.
1983. (1983-1984 Working Documents No. 902).

I 8.11   European Communities COM-Documents

In citing COM-Documents, give the COM-number as an
agency report number. Otherwise, it follows the standard
form, except that usually no imprint information is given on
the document.

> European Communities. Commission. *Financial*
> *Situation of the European Communities on 30 June 1981*
> (COM(81)400). n.p., [by 1981].

I 8.11a   In citing the microfiche edition, you should give the microfiche
number. You will also generally find more complete bibliographic data in this edition. Look for the information on the
microfiche frames, not on the header.

> European Communities. Commission. *Proposal for a*
> *Council Directive on Procedures for Harmonizing the Pro-*
> *grammes for the Reduction and ... Elimination of Pollu-*
> *tion ... from the Titanium Dioxide Industry*
> (COM(83)189 final; CB-CO 83 058-EN-C).
> Luxembourg: Office for Official Publications, 1983.
> (Microfiche EN-83-11).

I 8.12   Treaties of the European Communities

There are two classes of treaties of the European Communities:
the treaties which established the EC (i.e. the basic law of the
EC) and treaties between the EC and other parties.

I 8.12a   Establishing treaties should be cited by name, date, and
source. It is not necessary to give the parties because it must be
assumed that any EC member country has acceded to the
treaty.

> Treaty Establishing the European Economic Com-
> munity, signed in Rome on 25 Mar. 1957, *Treaties*
> *Establishing the European Communities* (FX-23-77-962-
> EN-C). 1978 ed. Luxembourg: Office for Official
> Publications, 1978.

I 8.12b   Treaties and agreements with other parties may be found in the *Collected Acts* (see I 7.3) and in other collections. Cite a title composed of the form of agreement and the subject; if none is given on the treaty, create one and enclose it in brackets. The title should be followed by the names of the parties and the date and place of signing or "doing." Finally, you should cite the source.

> [Agreement on Trade] between the European Economic Community and the Swiss Confederation, done at Brussels, 22 July 1972, pp. 18-31. In European Communities. Council. *Collection of the Agreements Concluded by the European Communities, Vol. 3: Bilateral Agreements EEC-Europe (1958-1975)* (RX-23-77-590-EN-C). Luxembourg: Office for Official Publications, 1978.

I 8.13   Working Documents of the Parliamentary Assembly of the Council of Europe

The working documents are published both separately and in collection.

I 8.13a   A citation to the collected working documents should include the number and date of the session and complete imprint information. These will be found on the title page. Since pagination starts over for each document, omit it; the document number is sufficient for location in the volume.

> Council of Europe. Parliamentary Assembly, 34th Ordinary Session, 26-30 Apr. 1982. "Report on the Defense of Democracy Against Terrorism in Europe" (Doc. 4878; 21 Apr. 1982), *Documents.* Strasbourg, 1982.

I 8.13b   A separate working document provides less information. You will find only the name of the issuing agency, a title and document number, and the date of publication. Use the day, month, and year. You may abbreviate the month, but do not use a number for it because there is too great a possibility for confusion between the American style (month/day/year) and the European style (day/month/year).

> Council of Europe. Parliamentary Assembly. *Report on Craftsmanship* (Doc. 4938). 20 July 1982.

I 8.14   **Official Report of Debates of the Parliamentary Assembly of the Council of Europe**

For a general debate, you do not need to give the names of the speakers. Begin with the name of the section and the pagination. (You do not need to name the part of the session or the volume number because, although there may be several volumes of debates in the session, the pagination is continuous.) Follow this with a full citation to the *Official Report*.

> "Science and Technology," pp. 628-656. In Council
> of Europe. Parliamentary Assembly, 33rd Ordinary
> Session. *Official Report of Debates* Vol. III.
> Strasbourg, 1982.

I 8.15   **Orders of the Day; Minutes of Proceedings of the Parliamentary Assembly of the Council of Europe**

Give the name of the section and the page numbers followed by a full citation. You must include the part number of the session with the issuing agency data. There will be more than one volume of *Orders* in each session, and the page numbers are not continous among them. You should also include, after the title, the number and date of the sitting.

> "Violence," pp. 63-64. In Council of Europe. Parlia-
> mentary Assembly, 34th Ordinary Session, 3rd Pt.
> *Orders of the Day: Minutes of Proceedings* 28th Sitting,
> 28 Jan. 1983. Strasbourg, 1982-1983.

Glossary

Act: a piece of legislation that has been approved by one chamber of the U.S. Congress. An Act becomes a Public Law after it has gone through the legislative process and is signed by the President. (Note: in some states laws are called Acts.)

Agency Report Numbers: unique numbers assigned to published documents. These numbers are alphanumeric and are usually located in the upper or lower corners of the cover and/or title page (see Fig. 7).

Agricultural Experiment Station/Agricultural Extension Service: agencies established by the U.S. Department of Agriculture, in cooperation with states, counties, and universities, to serve agricultural and rural communities.

ANSI (American National Standards Institute): an organization which attempts to set industry and engineering standards for various products. One group within ANSI deals with bibliographic standards.

Bibliographic Data Sheet: a form inserted in the front or back of technical reports, but also found in other document types. The standard sheet contains information on author(s), title, date, sponsoring and performing agencies, contract number, report number, subject headings, and abstract.

Bill: the most common form by which legislation is introduced in the U.S. Congress and state legislatures. In Congress all bill numbers are prefixed by H.R. or S. for House of Representatives or Senate, respectively.

Catalog: (v.) the process by which a library describes the physical makeup and intellectual contents of a book.

CIP (Cataloging in Publication): initial cataloging provided by the publisher when a book is printed. This information is usually located on the back of the title page and frequently is labeled "CIP."

Clearinghouses: organizations established primarily to provide copies of reports to individuals and groups.

COM-Docs: a class of documents submitted by the European Communities Commission to the Council of Ministers. These may be reports, proposals for action, etc. Until recently, they were not indexed and were difficult to obtain. In 1983, however, the EC began to issue them on microfiche with an index.

Committee Prints: written for Congressional committees, these publications provide background information on a piece of legislation or on a specific topic.

Conference Committee: a committee, composed of House and Senate members, which attempts to eliminate disagreements between Congressional chambers by reaching a compromise on a piece of legislation.

Conference Report: a report issued by a conference committee.

Contract Number: a series of numbers assigned to publications contracted for by the federal government. These numbers are usually alphanumeric but are not necessarily unique to a document. Therefore, they are not considered valid citation elements.

Cooperative Publications: documents which are jointly written and funded by more than one governmental or intergovernmental entity.

Documents: Congressional publications covering a variety of materials. Documents include committee activities, reports, communications to Congress from the President and other executive agencies, miscellaneous items from patriotic groups, annual reports to Congress, and reports from individual legislative fact-finding missions.

Ellipses: a form of punctuation (. . .) which indicates the omission of information. In citations, ellipses are usually employed when shortening title data.

ERIC (Educational Resources Information Center): a national network of 16 clearinghouses funded by the National Institute of Education. All publications available from ERIC deal with education and are identified by an agency report number beginning with ED.

European Communities: the Common Market, an economic, social, and, sometimes, political union of 10 Western European countries — France, Belgium, Denmark, Germany, Greece, Ireland, Italy, Luxembourg, the Netherlands, and the United Kingdom.

FBIS: see JPRS and FBIS.

Frame: an individual page in a microform. In microfiche the location of the frame is occasionally designated by an alphanumeric code (e.g., C5).

GPO (Government Printing Office): the printer to Congress and the major federal printer/distributor. The GPO is the agency responsible for the federal depository system, maintaining the SuDoc system and issuing the *Monthly Catalog of U.S. Government Publications.*

Grant Number: see Contract Number.

Hearing: a public meeting held by a Congressional committee to investigate a bill, to provide legislative oversight, or to gather background information on a particular issue. Also, the written testimony and discussion from such a meeting.

Imprint: a bibliographic term for the facts of publication — place of publication, publisher, and date of publication or copyright.

ISBN (International Standard Book Number): a unique multi-digit number which publishers assign to books. It is frequently used as an ordering and verification number by booksellers.

Item Numbers: numbers used by depository libraries to select federal publications. These numbers appear in the *Monthly Catalog of U.S. Government Publications,* preceded by the depository black dot. Since there is not necessarily a direct title to item number correspondence, these numbers are not included as citation elements.

JPRS (Joint Publications Research Service) and FBIS (Foreign Broadcast Information Service): translating agencies of the Central Intelligence Agency which monitor print and broadcast media worldwide.

Looseleafs: publications issued in a notebook format, which allows for easy updating. Frequently, pages are dated either at the top or at the bottom.

Mimeo: a document produced internally, usually by photocopying. Often identifiable by typewriter face.

Mimeo (UN): preliminary records of the UN General Assembly, Economic and Social Council, Security Council, and the Trusteeship Council. Many of them are later reissued as UN official records. They are identified by a series/symbol number and by the *lack* of a sales number or an official record designation.

NTIS (National Technical Information Service): a clearinghouse established within the U.S. Department of Commerce to distribute all forms of scientific, technical, and government-contracted reports.

Ordinances: laws of a municipality, passed by a municipal council or its equivalent. Such laws usually govern zoning, safety, building, noise, etc.

Parliamentary Body: used here to designate international groups which meet, debate, and pass resolutions, but which do not have legislative power (e.g., the UN General Assembly; Council of Europe Parliamentary Assembly; European Parliament).

Periodical: a title published at specified intervals (e.g., weekly, monthly).

Printer's Number: a number assigned by a printer when publishing documents. The number may be item specific or may be assigned to a number of documents printed on a particular day. Therefore, it is not considered a valid citation element.

Publication: any published material. This term is also used by some international organizations for works created especially for public sale (as opposed to documents or working papers). These works look like commercial press books and are treated as such by some libraries.

Public Law: the official name of a piece of legislation passed by the U.S. government. Each Public Law has a P.L. number designating the Congress and chronological order of passage (e.g., PL 97-235).

Readex Microprints: collections of government documents done by the Readex Corporation. Until 1984 the medium was micro-opaque cards; now they are on microfiche. UN Readex is filed by series/number; US Readex is filed by *Monthly Catalog* entry number.

Regulations: laws promulgated by executive agencies. They usually deal with the details of administering laws of legislative bodies.

Reports, Congressional: publications from a Congressional committee which recommend certain action, usually relating to a piece of legislation. Congressional reports present the committee's view of the legislative intent of a law.

Reprint: the republication of a document with no physical changes. Frequently, both the original and reprinting dates are listed on the document.

Resolution: a form of legislation in the U.S. Congress. Simple resolutions are designated by H.Res. or S.Res; concurrent resolutions by H.Con.Res. or S.Con.Res.; joint resolutions by H.J.Res. or S.J.Res.

Sales Catalogs: for some international organizations, these are the only listings of the publications of the organization. They may contain indexes — by subject, title, author — and/or they may be organized broadly by subject. They are usually available free from the agency or from its sales agent.

Serial Set: the official compilation of Congressional reports and documents. Each volume in the set is numbered on the spine of the volume. The set began in 1817.

Series/Symbol Number: a number assigned to a document by the UN. It indicates the issuing body, the type of document, and its place in the series.

Slip Law: the first official publication of a U.S. statute, issued as an unbound pamphlet. Slip laws give the text of a law, references to other statutes amended by the law, and a brief history of the bill's passage into law.

Sponsoring Agency: see Issuing Agency.

Star Print: a reprint of a piece of legislation, ordered because of typographical errors in the original publication. It is designated by a star in the lower left corner of the bill.

State Data Centers: institutions sponsored in cooperation with the U.S. Bureau of the Census and state governments. The objective of these centers is to provide census data more efficiently to groups, businesses, and individuals.

Stock Number: a twelve-digit number used by the GPO for ordering purposes. Because stock numbers have only recently appeared in indexes and have not been assigned to all GPO documents, they are usually not included in a citation.

SuDoc (Superintendent of Documents) System: an alphanumeric numbering system used by most federal depository libraries to classify federal documents. The system is arranged hierarchically by issuing agency.

Technical Report Documentation Page: see Bibliographic Data Sheet.

Title Page: usually the first printed page in a book or document. Information found on the front of a title page includes author, publisher, and title. The back of a title page contains the date and place of publication. With some documents the title page and cover may be the same.

UN Official Records: final records of the sessions of the UN. There are generally three types of official records: meetings record (verbatim or summary); supplements (reports, background material, etc.); and annexes (usually administrative information). Some official records do not fall into any of these classes.

University Press Books: books published by universities. Occasionally, university presses produce documents for the government.

Appendix A

Style Manuals

Brightbill, George D. and Wayne C. Maxson. *Citation Manual for United States Government Publications*. Philadelphia: Center for the Study of Federalism, Temple University, 1974.

Campbell, William Giles and Stephen Vaughn Ballou. *Form and Style: Theses, Reports, Term Papers*. 5th ed. Boston: Houghton Mifflin, 1978.

A Manual of Style. 13th ed. rev. Chicago: University of Chicago Press, 1982.

Modern Language Association. *MLA Handbook for Writers of Research Papers, Theses, and Dissertations*. New York: MLA, 1977.

Rothman, Marie H. *Citation Rules and Forms for United Nations Documents and Publications*. Brooklyn, N.Y.: Long Island University Press, 1971.

Turabian, Kate L. *A Manual for Writers of Term Papers, Theses, and Dissertations*. 4th ed. Chicago: University of Chicago Press, 1973.

A Uniform System of Citation. 13th ed. Cambridge, Mass.: Harvard Law Review Association, 1981.

U.N. Dag Hammarskjold Library. *Bibliographical Style Manual* (ST/LIB/ SER.B/8). New York, 1963.

U.S. Department of Justice. *A Style Manual for Machine-Readable Data Files and Their Documentation.* Washington: Government Printing Office, 1980. (J29.9:SD-T-3).

U.S. Library of Congress. Reference Department. General Reference and Bibliography Division. *Bibliographical Procedures & Style* by Blanche Prichard McCrum and Helen Dudenbostel Jones. Washington: Government Printing Office, 1954.

Van Leunen, Mary-Claire. *A Handbook for Scholars.* New York: Knopf, 1978.

Appendix B
Standard Government Document
Reference Sources

United States

American Statistics Index (ASI). Bethesda, Md.: Congressional Information Service.

Andriot, John. *Guide to U.S. Government Publications.* McLean, Va.: Documents Index.

CIS/Index to Congressional Publications. Bethesda, Md.: Congressional Information Service.

CIS U.S. Congressional Committee Hearings Index. Bethesda, Md.: Congressional Information Service.

CIS U.S. Congressional Committee Prints Index. Bethesda, Md.: Congressional Information Service.

CIS U.S. Serial Set Index. Bethesda, Md.: Congressional Information Service.

Congressional Index. Chicago: Commerce Clearing House.

Index to U.S. Government Periodicals. Chicago: Infordata International Inc.

Resources in Education. Phoenix, Ariz.: Oryx Press.

U.S. Bureau of the Census. *Census Catalog.* Washington: Government Printing Office.

U.S. Government Printing Office. *List of Classes of United States Government Publications Available for Selection by Depository Libraries.* Washington: GPO.

—————. *Monthly Catalog of U.S. Government Publications.* Washington: GPO.

U.S. National Technical Information Service (NTIS). *Government Reports Announcements and Index.* Springfield, Va.: NTIS.

United States Government Manual. Washington: Government Printing Office.

State, Local, Regional

Index to Current Urban Documents. Westport, Conn.: Greenwood Press.

U.S. Library of Congress. *Monthly Checklist of State Publications.* Washington: LC.

State Bluebooks and Reference Publications: A Selected Bibliography. Lexington, Ky.: Council of State Governments, 1983.

Statistical Reference Index (SRI). Bethesda, Md.: Congressional Information Service.

International

Documentos Oficiales de la Organizacion de los Estados Americanos. Washington: Organization of American States.

FAO Documentation. Rome: Food and Agriculture Organization of the United Nations.

Index to International Statistics (IIS). Bethesda, Md.: Congressional Information Service.

International Bibliography. New York: Unipub.

UNDOC. New York: United Nations.

UNESCO List of Documents and Publications. Paris: Unesco.

Yearbook of International Organizations. Brussels: Union of International Associations.

Index

Numbers refer to pages within Chapter 1. Alphanumerics refer to specific sections of Chapters 2–4. Italicized alphanumerics index only to specific examples of a bibliographic citation problem with no textual explanation.

135

Environmental impact statement,
  US 3.1a

EPA document, *US 1.1c*; *US 5.1a*

ERIC, US 4.2; *US 8.28b–8.28d*
  defined, see Glossary

Et al., US 2.6a; SLR 2.6a; I 2.6a

European Commission of Human
  Rights, I 8.7c

European Communities, *I 2.1b*;
  I 2.4–2.4a; *I 3.1a*; *I 4.2*; *I 6.2b*;
  I 7.1
  Collected Acts, I 8.12b
  COM-DOCS, I 8.11–8.11a
  defined, see Glossary
  Court of Justice Reports,
    I 8.7b
  European Parliament
    Debates, I 8.9d–8.9f
    working documents, I 8.10
  Official Journal, I 8.9–8.9g
  treaties, *I 7.3*; I 8.12–8.12b

European Court of Human Rights,
  I 8.7c–8.7e

Executive order, US 8.5; US 8.18

FAO, *I 1.1*; *I 1.2*; *I 5.1a*; *I 6.1c*
  microfiche, I 6.1a

FBIS report, US 8.26–8.26b

Federal Personnel Manual, US 6.1

Federal Register, US 8.5

Film, US 2.9; SLR 2.9; I 2.9; I 6.2c

Footnote
  abbreviated form, 9
  compared to bibliography, 8–9;
    Table 2
  content, 8
  form, Table 2
    citation to a part, 8
    citation to a periodical article, 8
    citation to a whole, 8
    second or later reference, 9

Foreign language
  see Language

Foreign Relations of the United States,
  US 8.16–8.16b

Freedom of Information Act material,
  US 8.32; SLR 8.12

Government Printing Office (GPO)
  as distributor, US 4.2; US 8.28e;
    US 8.29
  as publisher, US 4.2
  defined, see Glossary
  microfiche, *US 1.3f*; *US 2.9*;
    US 6.1; US 8.13c

Grant number, US 2.8
  defined, see Glossary

Greenwood microfiche, US 8.30b

Hearing, legislative, SLR 8.5c
  date of, US 2.5b–2.5c
  defined, see Glossary
  insert in, US 7.2
  title, US 2.1e
  see also Congress, U.S., hearing

House (U.S. Congress)
  see Congress, U.S.

House Journal, US 8.11

HUD Handbook, US 3.1b

IAEA, *I 4.1a*
  General Conference, *I 1.5c*
  proceedings, *I 7.2*

Ibid., 9

Idem, 9

IIS microfiche, *I 2.9*; I 6.1a

ILO, *I 7.2*
  conference, *I 1.5*
  microfiche, *I 2.9*

Imprint, US 4–4.3b; SLR 4–4.3b;
  I 4–4.3c
  defined, see Glossary

International Court of Justice Reports,
  I 8.7a

ISBN, I 6.2a
  defined, see Glossary

Issuing agency, US 1–1.3f;
  SLR 1–1.4b; I 1–1.5d
  abbreviation and acronym, I 1.3
  Congress as, US 1.3–1.3f
  geopolitical organization,
    SLR 1.1–1.1c